KING LEAR

My Reading

ARTHUR W. FRANK

KING LEAR
Shakespeare's Dark Consolations

OXFORD
UNIVERSITY PRESS

OXFORD
UNIVERSITY PRESS

Great Clarendon Street, Oxford, OX2 6DP,
United Kingdom

Oxford University Press is a department of the University of Oxford.
It furthers the University's objective of excellence in research, scholarship,
and education by publishing worldwide. Oxford is a registered trade mark of
Oxford University Press in the UK and in certain other countries

First Edition published in 2022

Impression: 1

Published in the United States of America by Oxford University Press
198 Madison Avenue, New York, NY 10016, United States of America

British Library Cataloguing in Publication Data
Data available

Library of Congress Control Number: 2021953357

ISBN 978-0-19-284672-3

DOI: 10.1093/oso/9780192846723.001.0001

Printed and bound in the UK by
Clays Ltd, Elcograf S.p.A.

SERIES INTRODUCTION

This series is built on a simple presupposition: that it helps to have a book recommended and discussed by someone who cares for it. Books are not purely self-sufficient: they need people and they need to get to what is personal within them.

The people we have been seeking as contributors to *My Reading* are readers who are also writers: novelists and poets; literary critics, outside as well as inside universities, but also thinkers from other disciplines—philosophy, psychology, science, theology, and sociology—beside the literary; and, not least of all, intense readers whose first profession is not writing itself but, for example, medicine, or law, or a non-verbal form of art. Of all of them we have asked: what books or authors feel as though they are deeply *yours*, influencing or challenging your life and work, most deserving of rescue and attention, or demanding of feeling and use?

What is it like to love this book? What is it like to have a thought or idea or doubt or memory, not cold and in abstract, but live in the very act of reading? What is it like to feel, long after, that this writer is a vital part of your life? We ask our authors to respond to such bold questions by writing not conventionally but personally—whatever 'personal' might mean, whatever form or style it might take, for them as individuals. This does not mean overt confession at the expense of a chosen book or author; but nor should our writers be afraid of making autobiographical connections. What was wanted was whatever made for their own hardest thinking in careful relation to quoted sources and specifics. The work was to go on in the taut and resonant space between these readers and their chosen books. And the interest within that area begins precisely when it is no longer clear how much is coming from the text, and how much is coming from its readers—where that distinction is no longer easily tenable because neither is sacrificed to the other. That would show what reading meant at its most serious and how it might have relation to an individual life.

Out of what we hope will be an ongoing variety of books and readers, *My Reading* offers personal models of what it is like to care about particular authors, to recreate through specific examples imaginative versions of what those authors and works represent, and to show their effect upon a reader's own thinking and development.

ANNE CHENG
PHILIP DAVIS
JACQUELINE NORTON
MARINA WARNER
MICHAEL WOOD

CONTENTS

PROLOGUE

A Tale of Two Families

One father, an aged king, convinces himself that his youngest daughter does not love him, though he loves her most. In his rage he exiles her. He then surrenders his royal powers and consigns his care to his two older daughters. Another father, noble but lesser in power, is duped by his younger son into believing that the elder is plotting against him. He orders his rightful heir to be hunted as a traitor. With the faithful children out of the way, the false children turn against their fathers, the false son aligned with the older daughters. The rejected children seek more than to serve their fathers; they seek to redeem them.

After much suffering, the two fathers are reunited with the children who have been true to them, but reconciliation is followed quickly by death. One father dies upon hearing the good news that his elder son lives and has, in disguise, been guiding his journey. The faithful daughter is murdered: a futile death, because her sisters are already dead, one killing the other and then herself.

The old king dies, saying 'Never, never, never, never, never . . .'

This book is a chronicle of going to the strangely ancient-but-contemporary world of *King Lear* and finding how that world does more than mirror aspects of my life. In *King Lear* I am offered words that can express what I could not say, and I come to know characters who show me aspects of myself that I could not acknowledge to be mine. My reading teaches me how to live with what is tragic, and how to believe in an unpredictable future.

1

VULNERABLE READING

How I read *King Lear* began in the early winter of 1986–87 when I was finishing chemotherapy to treat cancer. Relationships had become progressively strained. I had half forgotten the work I was doing before cancer and felt half embarrassed by what I remembered. Any life after illness was hard to believe in. Between treatments, I was sitting in our living room, unable to do anything but stare. I wasn't in pain, but I was flattened in every sense of my being. I was alone with memories of past mistakes that were my fault and with an illness that had nothing to do with fault. Together, these left me lost, with no feeling of a way forward.

So I just sat, and my good fortune was to have a room that invited staring. It was south facing and made the most of the winter sun. There were plants and pictures. One picture, given to me years before, was a poster from a Paris art exhibition of the stained glass windows of Marc Chagall, in which he depicted biblical scenes. This scene showed Jacob being blessed by the being that Chagall imagines as an angel. Jacob and this being have wrestled all night long. Neither can vanquish the other. Jacob is injured, but he refuses to let go until the angel gives him a blessing. It blesses him, renames him, and redirects his future (Genesis 32:22–32). Although how Jacob lives that future is another story.

As I stared at that picture, I realized I had been living my own variation of a very old story: a story shared by all those who encounter some force that is uncannily alien yet comes from within. This force is something that Jacob and all subsequent Jacobs must wrestle with; in this contest, they learn they cannot overcome it. Their long night's struggle ends with a wound and a blessing. Recognizing myself in Jacob's story, I felt part of a fellowship. The story did not tell me what to do; its consolation was to enable me to believe that I could do what was still to be discovered. My vulnerabilities remained, but a hint of possibility now shone through them, uncertain but open. Maybe most of all, and most difficult to explain, Jacob's story remained with me, as a companion I had not known I lacked. I have retold this story multiple times—it's there when I need it.

What happened to me that day was serendipity—a coming together not entirely by chance, but unplanned. This book attempts to make such encounters available as what you and I can seek, not merely wait for. Such encounters cannot be willed into happening—stories are not ours to command—but we can create conditions that invite their companionship.

The Edge of Vulnerability

I recovered from cancer, but I could not leave illness behind me. The study of illness experience and bioethics—the ethical dimension of healthcare, from clinical relationships to medical research—had been my academic interests since I was in graduate school in the 1970s. After illness turned overwhelmingly personal during the 1980s, these interests became truly a vocation for me.

Cancer was my second of two successive life-threatening illnesses, and these were followed immediately by the final illness and eventual death of my mother-in-law. My first book, *At the Will of the Body*, was a memoir of these years. Telling my story led to many people telling me theirs. Those stories were the basis of my second book, *The Wounded Storyteller*. I spent three decades trying to put into words the multiple sufferings caused by chronic and critical illnesses.

In the work of those decades, I tried to be a witness not only to people's sufferings with illness but also to their struggles to tell their own stories—that struggle is what my title, *The Wounded Storyteller*, calls attention to. But I neglected what my experience with Jacob's story taught me: that our human need to tell our own stories has a complementary need for stories that are *not* ours. This book explores that need. The figure whom I call the vulnerable reader is another side of the wounded storyteller; to be one requires being the other.

Vulnerable reading is how we read when some it threatens who we are committed to believing we are; it threatens the life we want to be able to continue to live. The threat may be immediate or in the future; obvious or vaguely sensed. *Vulnerable* is one of several words that I lean on heavily, including: *consolation*, *suffering*, *differences*, and *transcendence*. For the scope I want these words to have, each is better imagined than defined. To feel what I mean by vulnerability, I'll venture a Shakespearean metaphor.

In one of *Lear*'s most memorable scenes, the Earl of Gloucester has struggled to get to a cliff, intending to end his life by jumping. Vulnerability is finding ourselves suddenly placed on the edge of such a cliff, fearing what might push us over the edge. The bank we stand on could crumble, a gust of wind might throw us off balance, or prolonged dizziness might overcome us. Our fear is compounded by wondering whether we are desperate enough to jump.

Stories cannot and should not make these fears go away—the fears are realistic and useful for our survival. Stories can help us find a way to continue to stand on that edge and feel not secure but all right. All right not in the sense that it's a place we want to be, but in the assurance that it's a fully *human* place to be. Others have been here before; being here is our participation in a story we are part of, a story that was as unchosen for those who lived it in the past as it is for us now. Jacob's story forced my recognition that my pains, troubles, and continuing struggles were part of being fully human. Knowing I was playing my part in the continuing reenactment of an old story made all the difference: that's consolation.

Vulnerable reading is reading on the edge of a cliff, whatever it has brought us there. In vulnerable reading we seek a companion that can steady us, make our footing more firm, and then continue to be with us to turn to, confident it will offer assistance. But—and this qualification is crucial—companionship takes work on both sides. I had to already know Jacob's story for Chagall's picture to bring it alive in me. How I looked at the picture, and found myself in the story, was not passive. Stories require that we *make ourselves entitled to them*. This book is my attempt to make myself entitled to *King Lear*.

Enter Shakespeare

Shakespeare found me at another time in my life when I didn't know what I needed. I had become increasingly suspicious that I was repeating myself in what I wrote; hardly a crisis, but an impasse. Then we took a vacation to London, and my wife got tickets for several performances at the Globe, a theatre reconstructed to approximate Shakespeare's Globe, near the original location. Performances at the Globe don't allow you to sit back in the dark. You literally can't sit back: you're on a wooden bench, unless you're standing in the large pit that surrounds three sides of the stage thrust into it.

The Globe performance in which Shakespeare found me was *Measure for Measure*. The plot begins with the sudden imposition of strict enforcement of what have been unenforced laws. That leads to shutting down the city's brothels. In Shakespeare's day, the Globe was in a district filled with brothels, so that plot would have had an ironic humour. As the audience I was part of filled the courtyard, waiting to enter the theatre, actors in costume pushed their way between us carrying a small house on poles with two actors inside— it played the part of a brothel, rocking precariously. In this book, I want us to read like the not yet seated audience at *Measure for Measure*, finding ourselves pushed aside by the brothel's entrance.

The pre-performance scene in the Globe's courtyard was the opposite of a high-culture, worshipful Shakespearean performance: it was unexpected, rowdy, half improvised, and we were all part of it, whether we wanted to be or not. The play began in *action*, and when the action moved to the stage, interaction continued between the actors and the groundlings, those with cheap tickets who stand around the stage. The groundlings especially are part of the show. In a performance I saw of *Henry IV, Part I*, Falstaff reached down, helped himself to an audience member's glass of beer, drank what looked like a good deal, and eventually gave it back with thanks.

The Globe's *Measure for Measure* was a revelation for me, so different from the first Shakespeare play I can remember seeing, which was *King Lear*. We took a school trip to what was then a fine Shakespeare theatre in Stratford, Connecticut, built as a compromise between Elizabethan and modern design. I remember most the storm scene; I'd never seen an actor make tangible so much anger and pain. But as impressive as that performance was, our task was to sit quietly in the dark and admire what was performed up there. I departed more respectful than engaged.

After *Measure for Measure* we returned to the Globe for more plays. I downloaded the text of whatever we saw onto my phone and read Shakespeare as we travelled on London's Underground; the plays were perfectly at home being read there, usually standing, crowded among strangers, all of us trying to keep our footing as the train swayed. Then I wanted to read about the plays. I was down the rabbit hole, needing my daily Shakespeare. Pretty soon the questions I had long asked about illness found new responses. Shakespeare is always about how to live through suffering. Characters suffer in the comedies as much as in the tragedies; it just ends better for them, or seems to, for a while. Even the comic endings are tinged with an uncertain future. No present happiness is guaranteed to last. Shakespeare's consolations are, for me, more profound because they make no promises.

Beyond the Mirror of Our Troubles

Vulnerable reading most often begins by seeing how a story mirrors our own sufferings. In that reflection I reimagine suffering that had seemed uniquely mine, now knowing it is shared. The suffering reader and the suffering character in the story greet each other in a *you too* relation. But if reading stops at this mirroring, it risks becoming what the Shakespeare scholar Emma Smith calls 'narcissistic…reflecting back to us our own anxieties and preconceptions'.[1] Shakespeare should reflect back the anxieties of vulnerable readers—that's crucial to what makes Shakespeare valuable—but not in what Smith calls a narcissistic relation. In the Greek myth, Narcissus looks into a pool of water and sees only himself looking back. The mirror can become a trap: Narcissus drowns while trying to embrace his own image. That narcissistic vision is a risk of vulnerable reading. If we see in Shakespeare only what we bring initially to our reading, we make it all about us, and we will probably end up back where we started. Good companions do more than commiserate; they complicate who we think we are.

Back then during chemotherapy, as I thought about Jacob, I saw myself but I saw more than I wanted to recognize about myself. Jacob is a trickster: he has stolen his father's blessing from his brother, and he has stolen from his father-in-law, who has also tricked him. As I dwelled on Jacob's chequered past, he began to talk back to me, demanding to be more than a projection of how I felt. The story still reflected my anxieties and preoccupations, but it also unsettled them. Jacob may emerge blessed, but how he goes on to act is questionable to our ethical sensibilities; his transformation is fragmented, incomplete, a work in progress that sometimes goes backwards. Shakespeare's characters are as divided within themselves as Jacob. Like Jacob, they give me permission to recognize aspects of myself that I should remain uneasy about.

The best response to the risk of narcissism in vulnerable reading is offered by the theatre director Dominic Dromgoole, the artistic director of the Globe for over a decade. His warning addresses the inclination in vulnerable reading to move too quickly to see characters as reflections of our own troubles:

> Hamlet is not there to be the person we want him to be or to mollify our contemporary concerns; he is there to be Hamlet.[2]

Dromgoole reminds us that to get the story we are entitled to, we need to let the story and its characters be what they are. We have to go into their space and meet them, there. If we then import them into our space, the point is to reimagine our space through their eyes, not to make them see it our way, which would be bad companionship. *Imagination* is one word for describing the will to go to this strange world of characters who are not like us, and once there, to work out terms of companionship in which neither is who the other wants them to be.

Vulnerable reading begins with seeing my life mirrored in the story, but if I treat the story only as a mirror, that sells us both short: it fails to let the story be the companion that it can be, and it fails to ask me to become the companion that story is entitled to. What makes a story rich, or full, or whatever adjective of praise you want, is that it and its characters become better companions the more I provisionally leave my world and enter their world, rediscovering my concerns by seeing them framed in unfamiliar terms. Reading bounces back and forth between mirroring my world and the magical effect of taking me elsewhere, out of my point of view.

Why *King Lear*?

If the story that once lifted me out of my troubles and made itself my companion was biblical, and if the Globe's *Measure for Measure* was the performance that brought me out of my seat into the action, why is this book about *King Lear*? Because I needed, as a companion, a story about fathers, about the love between parents and children, and about the destruction that tensions between generations can bring about. My father celebrated his 101st birthday at the time I began writing this manuscript. He lives across the continent from me, alone in the house he and my mother moved to more than fifty years ago. My mother died when my father was ninety-three. During the years leading to his 101st birthday my visits had become more frequent and turned increasingly into care of my father, a significant part of which is care of his house as it too gets old, and exchanging many messages with those whom I hire to offer him direct care when I can't be there.

After my mother's death, my father undertook some projects that improved his life and others he could start but not finish; my wife and I had to pick up the pieces. As years passed, the disconnection between what I and professional caregivers believed he needed and what he insisted he could do for himself led to some difficult encounters. Reading *King Lear*, I once again felt the companionship of living my version of a very old story. Then my sense of connection shifted. The old man I saw reflected in Lear was myself as well as my father.

'Who is it that can tell me who I am?' (1.4.203), Lear asks in a moment of desperation as his identity is stripped away. My father asks me that question, in his own words, almost every evening when I call him. Slowly and reluctantly I realized I was asking that question myself. Old age makes Lear's question inescapable: I become less sure about the person I am becoming. *King Lear* shows me how to ask what to hold on to and what it is right to let go of, an issue my father and I share with most people our age. What parts of the person I have been should I continue to try to be? Behind that lurks the complementary question of what I have been in my younger life. Old age should be haunted by Lear's self-criticism, 'I have ta'en / Too little care of this' (3.4.35–6). I need a story that offers itself as a witness to the losses and uncertainty implied in having to ask myself who I now am; not a story to answer that question, but one that leaves open future possibility. *King Lear*, a story of two old men and their children, offers itself.

But here I remember Dromgoole's warning: Lear is not there to be an image of my father or of me. *King Lear* does mirror my troubles, but to see only that would be narcissism; it would miss the story's magic of taking us elsewhere. To reduce any of the characters in *Lear* to being who I want them to be treats them not as companions but as sidekicks. The sidekick walks a step behind, supporting, not questioning. A companion should provoke us, cause us to rethink what we need and what we ought to desire. *King Lear* provokes us in multiple ways, and those provocations give the play's eventual consolations their feel of truth, the truth of what we may need to hear, rather than what we want to hear.

Nor does *King Lear* reduce to being only about ageing and its twin threats of irrelevance and madness. *Nothing ever occurs one at a time* in Shakespeare. I like moments in the Shakespeare productions at the Globe when the actors who have been in one scene literally run off stage while those in the next scene enter, already speaking. Writing about the play is a struggle against separating too neatly what in the playing of the play runs on, overlaps, and interrupts. Chapters 2–6 of this book follow the play act by act, because arranging the chapters by thematic concerns risks reducing how enmeshed the familial and political, economic and emotional, mundane and transcendental are in *King Lear*. Shakespeare draws us into the maelstrom where these issues converge; from their entanglement he creates drama.

King Lear is about insiders who with terrible suddenness are shoved outside, and what they learn or don't learn from finding themselves positioned there. Some learn about power and what sustains it. Others learn about the riddle of what we call identity, and what props it up. Issues of power and identity are cross-cut by human vulnerability to deception. In the play's darkest moments of destructive rivalry and cruelty, characters' bodily suffering instigates their struggles against the limits of what language can express. All this begins with, and never stops being about, our human difficulty believing that we are loved and have a capacity to love.

I come to *Lear* with my own anxieties and preoccupations, not only the critical and chronic illness experiences that I lived myself and then studied for thirty years but also the political moment at which I write. You who read bring your own. The challenge in reading *King Lear* is to let Shakespeare speak to our troubles, but in his magical terms: to go far enough into his world for that to change how we experience our own. In the theatre we trust the actors who in turn trust Shakespeare's words. Those actors are making constant decisions about how to play their parts. Reading *King Lear*, we have to be actors and audience, both. We can't sit back in the dark and expect it to happen without our participation.

How Vulnerable Reading Reads

Vulnerable reading offers a reason to be reading—your life needs help. And it offers permission to read in whatever way does help.

Remember my starting point, that to know my own story, I need to encounter stories that are not mine. The metaphor *through the looking glass* might be most useful: I begin by seeing myself reflected, and then I try to move through that reflection to what Dromgoole means in the quotation earlier, when he writes that Hamlet is *there to be Hamlet*. Getting closer to who Hamlet is there to be in his story helps me figure out what I might be doing in my story. Even if vulnerable reading has no method—no prescribed steps to follow—it does follow a couple of basic principles, and these begin to explain why this book is organized as it is.

First, because vulnerability needs the solace of companionship, *read to develop relationships*. At the end of the reading, our relationships with characters continue, as they show us possibilities, and as they offer the simple reassurance that others have been here before, suffering the same. Because a story is the unfolding of relationships, I read *King Lear* by sticking to the story, watching how characters act and are acted upon, both how they change and how, despite changed circumstances, they remain the same. I seek to track my own reactions, as I progressively recognize what I see in them of myself, but also what I realize is not me. I may feel kinship or guilt in what I recognize about myself, and I may feel relief or envy in what is not me.

Second, *read for characters' vulnerabilities*. When characters recognize their vulnerability, how do they respond? Complementary to that, when do they fail to perceive they are vulnerable? What is at stake in how characters respond or fail to respond to vulnerability is their *identity*, but what does that much used word mean? On Shakespeare's stage and beyond, identity is specified in claims characters make for themselves: claims to what they believe themselves entitled to, and at the opposite end of the continuum, what they are willing to give up when their survival depends on that. The characters' claims are like my own in my life, always in flux as they are upheld, knocked down, or changed by how others treat us. Vulnerable reading looks at how people defend their identity, or else how they let go of who they have been, trusting to what they might become. *Lear* shows us both responses and what comes of them.

Third, how do characters *find consolation* in their suffering? Which consolations prove durable, and which are illusory? In *King Lear*, characters find consolation in their relationships to each other, especially when they offer forgiveness. They also console themselves in their use of language, as they express their pain and grief. But the play repeatedly questions the limits of what can be expressed. In its final words and images, we confront suffering beyond speaking. What is said is haunted by the shadow of the unsayable.

Fourth, I seek to *trust the words*. In Chapter 7, I talk about how Shakespeare's words achieve an independence, living outside the play in which they are spoken. As I hear words in the play, I anticipate how they might speak to me at some later time, responding to my need then. This book is formatted to emphasize phrases that command my attention. These words *make me* remember them: I place them as headings of sections within chapters. As these words and phrases come back to me in different moments of my life, *Lear* lives in me, or I in it.

These principles are useful points of entry, but I remind myself that consolation has most often come as a surprise, as in the moment with the Chagall image of Jacob. In my life and in the lives I've seen around me, planned consolations often disappoint. Consolations come more often in fragments that are unbidden, though not unprepared for. Vulnerable reading is *a way of preparing ourselves* to recognize what consoles, when it comes. Thus the issue for this book is not whether *King Lear* consoles you, the reader of this book. The issue is whether spending time with *Lear* can prepare you for what will. I intend this book to be a field manual for gathering fragments that can someday console.

2

THE UNRAVELLING

'I'll tell thee thou dost evil.' (1.1.172)

What if love and evil do not sit poles apart, the one a safe haven from the other?

In Shakespeare's world, love and evil seem always there, irruptive forces both, waiting upon conditions.

If in some moment love is frustrated, it turns against itself.

Evil waits upon such moments.

How does what seems so solid and stable—a life or a state—so readily fall apart? The first vulnerability is believing in your own invulnerability. Lear is he upon whom others wait. His entrance is anticipated by his chief courtiers, Kent and Gloucester, uncertain what he will do. The court expects him to announce who will succeed him and to declare who will marry his youngest daughter, Cordelia: the Duke of Burgundy or the King of France. Lear dispatches Gloucester to bring them forward; kings are his to summon. I see someone one step from the edge of a precipice he cannot perceive.

'we shall express our darker purpose'

'Meantime we shall express our darker purpose' (1.1.34), Lear announces to the expectant court, and my reading begins in uncertainty about what darkness is foretold on a day that should celebrate peaceful succession and happy marriage. Lear's words may look further ahead than he can see. But we have no time to reflect, because Lear disrupts the ceremony that has just begun. His statement starting in the middle of a line like a casual interjection, Lear demands his daughters to tell him 'Which of you shall we say doth love us most' (1.1.49). I doubt Lear's darker purpose lies in what he imagines this test will reveal; I doubt he has any doubts what will be revealed. The map dividing the kingdom is already drawn. Most likely, Lear wants a final moment to toy with his power to dispense.

Shakespeare's original audiences would have known variations of the folktale about a king who coerces his daughter to declare her love for him. In one version, he demands his daughter marry him—that's a darker purpose. She escapes. The princess in the version of the story closest to *King Lear* answers her father with a riddle, saying she loves him like salt. Her wit is beyond the king; enraged, he banishes her. The princess marries a prince who recognizes her inherent nobility, and eventually she arranges for her father to rediscover her. She serves him a dinner with no salt in the cooking. When he comments on how tasteless the food is, she observes the value of salt; he is enlightened, realizing how he failed to recognize the expression of love in the answer he rejected. Shakespeare borrows this old story—the king's failure to recognize love sets the plot in motion—but with his own darker purpose. The expectation of the folktale's happy ending is deceptive.

Lear commands his daughters to declare their love beginning with the oldest, then middle, and finally youngest, thus setting up Cordelia's triumph, which will reflect his glory as father and king. Goneril and Regan play their parts with words of nonspecific effusiveness. Lear then addresses Cordelia: 'Now our joy...what can you say to draw | A third more opulent than your sisters'?' (1.1.81, 84–5). He frames love as performance and performance as acquisition.

'Love and be silent'

'What shall Cordelia speak?' she asks in an aside, while her sisters give their speeches. Her answer is: 'Love and be silent' (1.1.60). For me, Cordelia's 'love and be silent' recalls the opening lines of the Chinese book of wisdom, the *Tao Te Ching*, attributed to the quasi-mythical Lao Tzu. One translation begins: 'The Tao that can be told is not the eternal Tao. The name that can be named is not the eternal name.' Or, more colloquially: 'The name you can say isn't the real name.'[1] Some things not only exceed language but are diminished if forced into language: the effusiveness of Goneril and Regan diminishes the love they proclaim. The unordinary language of the *Tao*, and of Shakespeare, says while calling attention to the limits of what can be said. Such language is double voiced, commenting on itself, offering while disclaiming what is offered.

Cordelia's problem is my problem writing this book, the problem of anyone who needs a word to express more than any word can bear. What I name as vulnerability, or as suffering, or as consolation is more than those words can contain: what I name are not the real names. What I will call transcendence is especially not its real name.

When Lear again asks Cordelia what she will say to gain this greatest share, she answers 'Nothing, my lord' (1.1.86). Nothing, that is, if speech is framed as gain. That word *nothing* repeats like a refrain throughout the play, calling upon us to take seriously what *nothing* actually is; no thing, no word, no representation. Silence is nothing, but silence is not pure absence; silence is that from which speech is born and to which it returns. Silence is patience, the virtue Lear asks the gods to grant him but may never find. Questions multiply: Is *nothing* only as Lear seems to imagine it: a void, empty, cold, and fathomless? Or is *nothing* the primal possibility of all that can be? Is *nothing* the absence of love, or can *nothing* be the limit at which language must cease, lest it substitute itself for what is loved? And when nothing is spoken, what does that silence risk?

Cordelia's 'Nothing, my lord' implicitly poses a riddle: what is silent but eloquent, empty but full, and faithful by being disobedient? Lear can only reply that 'Nothing will come of nothing: speak again' (1.1.89).

By now Lear feels vulnerable: no longer giving away his daughter and his kingdom but rather losing both. He offers Cordelia another chance to speak, but he again frames what she will say in the language of acquisition: 'Mend your speech a little, / Lest you may mar your fortunes' (1.1.93–4). Cordelia herself adopts Lear's economic register, and that renders her speech cold, distant. 'I love your majesty / According to my bond, no more nor less', she says (1.1.91–2). That word *bond* echoes Shylock in *The Merchant of Venice*. Shylock's bond is the legal contract according to which the merchant Antonio promises a pound of his flesh if he does not repay Shylock's loan by a specified date. When Shylock anticipates that Antonio will default on the loan, he repeats three times: 'Let him look to his bond' (*Merchant of Venice*, 3.1.32–4). In the trial scene, when Shylock is pressed to offer mercy, he answers: 'I stay here on my bond' (*Merchant of Venice*, 4.1.243). By then, the *bond* has become a nonhuman actor requiring humans to act as it dictates; such nonhuman actors are haunting presences on Shakespeare's stage.

The haunting presence of this nonhuman actor, the bond, leads me to ask whether Lear's darker purpose is another nonhuman actor. Lear is making mistakes, certainly, but perhaps the darker purpose exceeds his willed intention. Are we humans vulnerable to falling into the grip of purposes that are uncanny in being both ours and not ours? Lear speaks the demand for performances, but the purpose may be making him its vehicle.

'So young and so untender?' Lear pleads with Cordelia. 'So young, my lord, and true', she replies (1.1.106–7). *True* here means faithful, constant, authentic. Cordelia is always *truly* Lear's daughter. Her response to him does on her own terms exactly what he calls upon her to do: best her sisters in a competition of performances. But instead of fulfilling Lear's expectation that she exceed her sisters in the language of flattery, she exceeds them in speaking with a depth of recognition—the recognition of how speech distorts love—that they cannot comprehend. The problem is that Lear can't comprehend it either. Cordelia wins, but on terms only she can understand. She knows Lear cannot understand, yet she goes ahead anyway, risking so much; why?

Cordelia may have her own darker purpose, or again, a darker purpose may have her, and that makes her tragic. Yet her purpose, unlike Lear's, is specific; it is what her actions will eventually bring about: battle with her sisters, with the prize being Lear himself. Here I find the first instance of a recurring question about several characters: how far ahead can Cordelia see? She could have avoided so much by playing her father's game, giving him enough of what he wants. The grey space between principle and self-righteousness is the ground of tragedy. Cordelia raises the stakes in the competition Lear sets up: she wants not to say that she loves her father the most; she wants to show it—in blood.

I hear this darker purpose in Cordelia's last words in Act I; she will not reappear until Act IV. She addresses her sisters and again marks the limit of what she will speak, though this time because any name would fall short of expressing how malign the objects of her speech are:

> Cordelia leaves you. I know you what you are.
> And like a sister am most loath to call
> Your faults as they are named.
> . . .
> Time shall unfold what plighted cunning hides.   (1.1.284–6, 296)

My reading is skewed by having seen too many family dramas of competition over who most loves someone, generally a parent or grandparent, and who is loved the most by that person. But all hell is about to break loose, and that's not unforeseeable to Cordelia. A very great deal must be at stake for her not to prevent it.

My reading is also affected by many stories about the moment when a physician tells someone the bad news of a diagnosis of critical illness, and having been forced to play those scenes myself. People being diagnosed with potentially incurable illnesses share Cordelia's dilemma: the diagnostic label cannot name all that they feel themselves losing, nor can their need in this moment be adequately spoken. So they grieve and remain silent. What such moments call for is shared silence, but that is what institutional medicine is least able to provide. Too many healthcare professionals act in accordance with Lear's expectation that language can express whatever is felt. 'Do you have any questions?' they ask, which is well intentioned but assumes that patients can specify their needs in words and whatever exceeds those words is nothing, in Lear's sense.

Physicians are haunted by fears of mistakes or inadequacy. Those fears lead them to avoid patients—the Cordelias of the clinic—who confront them with what they cannot name, chart, and control. In Lear's court as in the clinic, power needs to presume the adequacy of names that the powerful apply, and power must banish claims that the name you can say is not the real name. Those who, like Cordelia, confront this power, feel their only choice is silence.

'What woulds't thou do, old man?'

'What wouldst thou do, old man?'(1.1.148), Kent asks Lear, protesting Cordelia's banishment. Hearing Kent's plea for Lear to stop and reflect is when I first realized what a resonant companion *King Lear* is to me at this stage of my life. Watching the breakdown between Kent and Lear takes me to the edge that I was on many times with my father. In the years after my mother's death, he made unilateral decisions I believed to be questionable both for his own best interest and for us, his family. My objections were dismissed, but the consequences fell on me to deal with.

What wouldst thou do, old man? is the cry of whoever struggles to care for a parent who needs that care but who makes it difficult for others to enact it. Kent, Cordelia, and especially Edgar are the patron saints of so-called adult children, a euphemism I increasingly resent for its failure to recognize that some of us are elderly ourselves. My father is no Lear. He has never cursed or exiled me. But Lear's rejection of Kent's efforts to save him from himself is a moment in which I see my frustrations. Then I ask what else I should be seeing.

I resisted realizing I had the ages wrong: I am closer by far to Lear's age. Kent later tells us he's 48, young enough to be my son. Lear's age of four score plus is within a decade of mine. In my care for my father, I am expected to play Kent's role so often that it's a shock to realize I am more accurately Lear. So now I ask of myself, 'What wouldst thou do, old man?'—or more often I forget to ask those words until after I need them. My reading thus finds itself on both sides of a generational divide: the two generations' love for each other totters on the edge of conflict, sometimes falling over that edge.

Lear defines himself by acts of rejection: 'Come not between the dragon and his wrath' (1.1.123), he warns Kent. Lear believes that playing the dragon sustains him. He cannot see how that performance shuts him off from Kent's good council and, worse, from Cordelia. 'I loved her most, and thought to set my rest / On her kind nursery' (1.1.124–5), Lear says, some part of himself realizing what he cannot stop himself from doing. What performances, I ask myself, am I committed to sustaining, at what cost?

While the bitterness of Lear's two rejections of love still hangs in the air, Shakespeare offers us a rare moment when love can speak and be true. Burgundy and France enter. Lear informs them that he has disowned Cordelia: she no longer inherits any lands or other wealth. Who wants her now? Burgundy decamps. France turns commodity and exchange into metaphor, his usage restoring the primacy of lives over lands: 'She is herself a dowry,' he declares

(1.1.254). France will not reappear, but in his moment, he is a great lover.

'He hath ever but slenderly known himself'

Goneril and Regan don't gloat. They realize Lear never imagined himself stepping down, but only taking a step to one side, without abdicating the privileges of kingship. The sisters plot tentatively, still unsure. Again I hear them through my own experience of families, in this instance older siblings' resentment that the parent loves the youngest best. 'He always loved our sister most,' Goneril says, but she then adds: 'and with what poor judgment he hath now cast her off appears too grossly' (1.1.306–7). That may express less sympathy for Cordelia than apprehension of the trouble to come when Lear realizes his mistake. Regan proposes Lear's age as an excuse for his behaviour, but then rejects that: ''Tis the infirmity of his age: yet he hath ever but slenderly known himself' (1.1.308–9).

He hath ever but slenderly known himself. On my reading, *King Lear* is as much about what difference old age does *not* make as it is about the effects of aging. Personal dispositions do not appear suddenly in old age. They become accentuated, and age too often gives people a sense of license to act out what has always been their worst side. The grumpiness of my own old age is new only in how I indulge it. Goneril affirms Regan's judgement: 'The best and soundest of his time hath been but rash.' Lear's current behaviour is nothing new, but rather 'imperfections of long-engrafted condition' (1.1.310–12), a phrase I quote often, about myself and others. The metaphor of grafting, which I associate with plants, describes so well how some external demand for action or feeling grows into us until it is part of our being. Old age is when the accumulation of long-engrafted imperfections becomes all too visible. Youth is wanting to become yourself, still discovering who you might be. Old age is having to see exactly who you have become, or it is being unable to see the consequences of who you cling to being. Lear imagines himself as the dragon. To his daughters, he acts on the same slender self-knowledge as always.

The sisters agree they must act quickly, but they have as yet no plan, only a tacit alliance in how they will react to whatever Lear does. My temptation to feel any affinity with them is already fading. The insight they show about their father makes their later treatment of him more evil, because they are smart enough to know better. But they too act from long-engrafted conditions, although Shakespeare gives us only hints as to what these are.

'Nothing like the image and horror of it'

King Lear reads as if it were a musical composition of variations on themes that blend and reinforce each other. One theme is the opening of chaos: the void created by Lear breaking down order, ceremony, and authority. Goneril and Regan are the first variation of what fills the chaos that Lear's rage has opened, an intimation of evil. A second variation is Edmund, the bastard son of Gloucester. If the sisters' designs are vaguely hinted at, Edmund's plan is fully premeditated. He enters with a bravura that comes as a breath of fresh air in the claustrophobic spaces of the scenes at court. He seduces by playing the underdog with a claim to speak for the oppressed.

In the opening scene Gloucester treats Edmund's birth as a bastard as if it were Edmund's deficiency, rather than the result of Gloucester's own behaviour. Now Edmund speaks for anyone marginalized by accident of birth. His soliloquy confronts us with a good question: What justice can there be in his brother, Edgar, getting all the land and titles just because he was born 'some twelve or fourteen moonshines' sooner and was begat with Gloucester's legal wife? 'Why brand they us / With base?' (1.2.9–10). By the time Edmund's speech reaches its punchline, 'Now, gods, stand up for bastards!' (1.2.22), I too feel plagued by custom (1.2.2–3) and ready to cheer him on. But then his father enters, Edmund's plot begins to unfold, and another moment of sympathy implodes.

Again, *nothing* is that from which all follows. As Gloucester enters, Edmund makes a show of concealing a letter. Gloucester asks what it is. 'Nothing, my lord' (1.2.31) is the evasive answer, calling attention to what it conceals. Edmund has forged the letter to appear to be written by Edgar. The forged letter convinces Gloucester because it expresses what he fears might be true: 'I begin to find an idle and fond bondage in the oppression of aged tyranny, who sways, not as it hath power, but as it is suffered' (1.2.47–9). Gloucester has just seen 'the oppression of aged tyranny' in Lear's treatment of Cordelia and Kent. The letter exploits his fears that in his own old age his power no longer reflects his capacities as a just lord and leader. Instead, others jolly him along, and their sufferance can be readily withdrawn. Gloucester's self-doubt is his vulnerability. Edmund's forged letter makes explicit the play's meditation on authority and power: when allegiance is well earned versus when it is compelled by oppression.

The story of Gloucester, Edmund, and Edgar has been called a sub-plot in *King Lear*. I can't see anything *sub* about it. In *Lear* stories proceed in parallel, sometimes converging, and fully merged in the ending. Each story is another aspect of the other. I resist saying that each completes the other, because in *King Lear* nothing ever seems complete, if that means wrapped up and finished. Better to say that each story, so far as the stories are separable, broadens the implications of the other, expanding its reach.

Even in Edmund's moment of seeming invulnerable, his words look further than he can see, as Lear's did earlier. Now convincing Edgar that their father is angry with him, Edmund says: 'I have told you what I have seen and heard, but faintly, nothing like the image and horror of it' (1.2.151–3). *Nothing like the image and horror of it.* Cordelia could say 'nothing like' the love she felt; now Edmund claims language fails at making horror immediate. He's lying, but then his words step off the page and the phrase takes on a life of its own. I think of how journalistic reports of the world's troubles convey nothing like the image and horror of it. In this moment of deceptive speech, truth is spoken.

Edmund, now alone, does gloat: 'A credulous father and a brother noble, / Whose nature is so far from doing harms / That he suspects none' (1.2.156–8). True as far as it goes: Gloucester is credulous and Edgar too noble to suspect his brother. But the easy accomplishment of Edmund's deception depends on more than the susceptibility of these particular victims. Shakespeare reminds me how fragile we humans are in what we name with words like *self* and *identity*. Identity is a house of cards: like power, it exists only 'as it is suffered'. The powerful may be no more haunted by knowing this than the rest of us are; only the stakes are different. Edmund needs to do so little to make his father and his brother see threat where they believed there was affection. Lear is so easily unfixed by Cordelia not going along with his plan. He fears that he is not loved but merely suffered.

Lear and Gloucester both respond to whatever makes their vulnerability explicit by seeking to make it disappear: Cordelia is banished; Edgar is proclaimed an outlaw. Both old men repress their sense of vulnerability, thus turning it into a self-fulfilling prophecy.

'What's that? / Authority'

Goneril complains: 'By day and night he wrongs me... His knights grow riotous, and himself upbraids us / On every trifle' (1.3.4, 7–8). The time elapsed must be less than a month, because Lear is in his first residence with his elder daughter, and what he cobbled together in haste and anger is already falling apart. What Lear gave his daughters, he then half took back, proclaiming he would live with Goneril and Regan alternately, a month at a time. He invested his sons-in-law, Albany and Cornwall, with his 'power, / Pre-eminence, and all the large effects / That troop with majesty' (1.1.131–3). But, Lear retained 100 knights—a small army, including their servants—to be housed and fed by his daughters during his alternating residences. How far any stage production actually shows the knights being riotous—or not—affects how we hear Goneril. In one famous production, they literally broke up the furniture. That makes sense, if we remember that Lear doesn't want to be there; the knights act out his unhappiness over what has happened.

Thus when Goneril instructs Oswald, her senior household manager and confidant, to 'Put on what weary negligence you please' in serving Lear (1.3.13), she is not being unreasonable. I love *weary negligence* for the threat implied in such euphemistic under-statement. Yet in that threat Goneril begins to be terrifying. It's a line an actor can play, or a reader can hear, foreboding of when negligence will turn active.

Elsewhere in the household, Lear interviews Caius, who seeks employment. 'Dost thou know me, fellow?' (1.4.25), Lear asks. He should be asking himself if he recognizes Caius, who is Kent in disguise, having defied the order of exile and returned to serve Lear as he still can. I cannot share the difficulty some commentators have believing that Kent could disguise himself so as to be unrecognizable to people who knew him so well. *King Lear* presents failures of recognition as a human condition: Lear can't recognize Cordelia's love; Gloucester loses sight of who Edgar is. In this world of misrecognitions, Kent's ability to pass himself off as Caius is frightening in its credibility.

Kent deflects the question, telling Lear he has 'that in your countenance which I would fain call master.' 'What's that?' asks Lear. 'Authority,' Kent replies (1.4.26–9), opening another variation on the question raised in Edmund's forged letter: When is authority earned and when is it merely suffered? Kent speaks to the necessity of authority, as surrounding events show authority made fragile through misuse. Kent hopes to remind Lear of who he was and might be again, and he reminds us that authority has two faces. Authority can be 'the oppression of aged tyranny'; Gloucester buckles because he recognizes the truth in that phrase. But authority can also be what Kent works to sustain in Lear; the capacity of leadership to keep chaos at bay. At least, the possibility of such authority is Kent's fragile hope.

Kent's belief, closer to a faith, in true authority matches his belief in true speech. Both beliefs are part of a life lived without a trace of irony. When Kent addresses Lear as 'old man', he justifies his lack of deference with the claim: 'To plainness honour's bound / When majesty falls to folly' (1.1.150–1). Yet Kent's words are often double voiced, their significance exceeding his intention. Shakespeare embeds messages in Kent's plain speech. Thus when Oswald's weary negligence in serving Lear crosses the threshold of offence, Kent-as-Caius attacks Oswald, saying: 'I'll teach you differences' (1.4.84). A footnote to most editions of the play explains *differences* as referring to class distinctions. Oswald has gotten above himself. But *differences* is another word like *authority* and *nothing* that gains significance as it is repeated. All the characters need to learn about differences, except perhaps the Fool, who now enters. He understands differences quite well already. Lear, especially, has to learn differences not only in class and privilege but in power and authority, in love and the expression of truth, and in human's relation to the gods. *King Lear* teaches us differences.

'Dost thou know the difference . . .'

Another variation is now played, this one on forms of truth telling. Cordelia expresses truth in silence; Kent believes in plain speaking. The Fool knows how Lear can tolerate truth being told: elliptical, half joking, half mad. He tells Lear the truth first in a straightforward metaphor—'thou mad'st thy daughters thy mothers: for when thou gav'st them the rod and put'st down thine own breeches'

(1.4.146–8)—but then switches into a nursery rhyme before Lear angers:

> Then they for sudden joy did weep.
> And I for sorrow sung.
> That such a king should play bo-peep
> And go the fool among.   (1.4.149–52)

The Fool always seems one step ahead, until he gets lost entirely.

The Fool's set-up to one of his joking riddles echoes what Kent has just said about teaching differences: 'Dost thou know the difference, my boy, between a bitter fool and a sweet one?' (1.4.129–30). Before we hear the punchline, that joke changes into another one, and the difference seems to be left untold, hanging, as it were. Maybe the answer is the Fool himself, both bitter and sweet: a conjunction of opposites.

As much as I admire Cordelia and Edgar, as much as Lear arouses my sympathy, it's to the Fool that my heart goes out, in his clarity, his faithfulness, and his vulnerability. I study not to be the Fool, but to share his perspective: standing below as he does, he literally understands as no other character does. My affection may have begun when I read the part of the Fool one evening at a small conference. The organizer decided that we would stop talking about bioethics and do a readers' theatre, reading *King Lear* with assigned parts that we spent the briefest time rehearsing. Even performing an abridged version, seated, felt like a marathon. But it gave me at least an intimation of what actors describe: the power of experiencing Shakespeare's words as your own. Both your words and not at all your words—the Fool could turn that into a riddle.

In this interlude with the Fool, Lear has his final moment of being among those whose service to him is unqualified. His descent now begins in earnest.

'Who is it that can tell me who I am?'

The house of cards that is Lear's identity collapses. 'Are you our daughter?' (1.4.192). Lear asks Goneril, his irony forcing the issue of disrespect. But it's Lear's own sense of who he is that is threatened:

> Does any here know me? This is not Lear.
> Does Lear walk thus? Speak thus? Where are his eyes?
> Either his notion weakens, his discernings
> Are lethargied—Ha! Waking? 'Tis not so?
> Who is it that can tell me who I am?   (1.4.199–203)

To that closing question—*Who is it that can tell me who I am?*—the Fool replies with perhaps his finest phrase: 'Lear's shadow'. That confronts Lear with what he most fears: becoming a form of *nothing*. For Lear, that fear is justified. Yet when I was once forced into being my own shadow, I learned to cultivate what can be seen from that perspective.

For decades I have based my work on a simple act of imagination: to return to the lowest moment when I was being treated for cancer, when I seemed to have lost all I valued about myself and all I thought gave me standing among others. When I felt, in the Fool's phrase, that I was a shadow of who I had been. Then, very gradually, that perspective became enabling: no longer having a stake in upholding anything, I could ask what the world's priorities and practices are, how we allocate kindness and care. But I was younger then than Lear is. And I recall this in retrospect. The possibilities in being my own shadow became apparent only when my shadow self regained sufficient substantiality. The first moments of being your own shadow are desolate, terrifying.

In Lear's desperate plea, *Who is it that can tell me who I am?*, I hear myself in those lowest moments, and I hear every ill person I have listened to during these last decades, asking who they now are, and if they have a future, who they could be again. The question hopes for an answer but fears there can be none, that's its desperation. Lear is desperate: 'Thou shalt find / That I'll resume the shape which thou dost think / I have cast off for ever' (1.4.282–4), he threatens. But he won't. Shakespeare shows us how a person falls apart: what Lear calls his 'notion', his ability to understand, weakens; 'his discernings', his ability to tell differences, have been lost. He fears that no one can tell him who he is because he is nothing.

Lear's cry speaks to and for the vulnerable reader, yet his lines do more than mirror despair. Hearing Lear, vulnerable readers begin to believe that someone *can* tell them who they are: Shakespeare can. Lear's words offer to those who ask the same question the companionship of souls equally lost, the fellowship of the unrecognized. Lear's shadow can be the beginning of someone else's self-recognition.

'Darkness and devils!'

'Darkness and devils!' (1.4.222) is Lear's most polite expression of frustration. The curses that he has been hurling at Goneril become more violent:

Dry up in her the organs of increase,
And from her derogate body never spring
A babe to honour her: if she must teem,
Create her child of spleen, that it may live
And be a thwart disnatured torment to her.   (1.4.252–6)

Lear's curses on Goneril's future fertility have the obvious symmetry that he is offended by his own 'child of spleen'. But Lear's curses are misogynistic, intolerably vicious whatever their cause. As these curses are repeated, later directed at Regan, they suggest what is the sisters' long-engrafted condition. Lear elicits my sympathy as I watch all the attendance, the deference, the trappings of majesty that have affirmed who he is being wrenched away. Yet I am equally horrified by how his curses reveal too much about the one who utters them. I hope Lear's curses tell me more about the character Shakespeare is creating than about Shakespeare.

'Thou shouldst not have been old till thou hadst been wise' (1.5.39–40), the Fool half jokes. How quickly we get old, and how slowly we become wise. Lear, speaking to no one in particular, utters another of his cries of imminent loss: 'O, let me not be mad, not mad, sweet heaven!' (1.5.41). What he has already done is madder in its consequences than anything he will do, but the madness was never his alone. Save for Kent, the Court stood by and let Lear act the dragon. Thus the world enables the perversion of authority. In *King Lear*, no one person is ever solely responsible. Madness and responsibility are both real but distributed, never one person's alone. Shakespeare's art is to balance inner chaos and external affliction, as each responds to the other.

'I did her wrong—,' Lear says (1.5.22), another non sequitur in the middle of one of the Fool's jokes. Self-divided as always, he quickly disavows that realization, lapsing back into self-justification: 'So kind a father!' (1.5.29). Actions rebound upon the actor. Lear's deepest suffering is knowing that if he did not strictly cause what is beginning to happen, his participation is tangled in the root of it. What *have I done*, old man, I ask myself. What do I continue to do? Whom do I misrecognize? How in defending the house of cards that is my identity do I turn my vulnerabilities into self-fulfilling prophecies? Old age itself unravels aspects of a life with the toll that years exact upon bodies. *King Lear* shows people's own participation in this unravelling.

3

THE REFUGE OF SECOND SELVES

'Edgar I nothing am.' (2.2.187)

An old man and a young man each has his identity stripped away: the younger all at once, the older piece by piece.

Edgar, made suddenly desperate, accepts the annihilation of who he has been.

Lear, who has ever but slenderly known himself, clings to what he cannot give up.

Where to run, and who must you become, to fit the places where you shelter? In a recurring Shakespearean plot, threatened characters turn into second selves, at first only to hide in disguise, but then to explore new possibilities of who they can be. At the end of comedies, I'm sorry to see characters return to being the self that they had to give up; the second self—often a cross-gendered self—was freer, funnier, more open to whatever comes along. *Lear*'s characters vary in what they do with the possibilities offered by being a second self. Cordelia, returning as the avenging warrior queen, is less a second self than a hardened version of who she has always been, empowered by the army behind her, then defiant in defeat. Kent in disguise as the servant Caius does little to explore being what Kent the Earl could not be. But Gloucester's second self, blinded and turned out of his house, becomes able to regret much about who he was; with Edgar's help, he claims to see differently. Lear's second self takes the form of madness in which he finds, briefly but memorably, a political clarity that his primary self was incapable of. That leaves Edgar and his second self. My reading of Act II hinges on Edgar's fateful decision to become Poor Tom.

When Emma Smith, one of my favourite contemporary Shakespeareans, writes of 'the colourless Edgar', I wince.[1] Not because Smith is wrong: Edmund is more colourful than Edgar, and *King Lear* does turn increasingly monochromatic in Act II. But in my reading, Edgar isn't there to be colourful. Edgar is there to show what it costs him to survive—his will to survive—and how far he can win for himself a sustainable survival after all he suffers. In my vulnerable reading, I see in Edgar the situation of ill people who have to undergo far more violent and prolonged medical treatments than I went through. Edgar survives by willing himself to be someone utterly different. He accepts the pain and degradation that goes with being that person, and he finds in that second self a task, a mission that enables him to *become*. That verb could have several predicates: a truer son, an avenging brother, eventually a king. But these predicates seem only part of what Edgar may become. At the play's end, what Edgar becomes is another story we're left to imagine. Shakespeare makes us believe in that possible story. In that belief, vulnerable reading finds consolation.

'I will preserve myself'

Edmund railed against being called base because of his illegitimate birth. In Act II Edgar assumes baseness in order to stay alive. Until now, Edgar's words have been limited to compliant responses to Edmund. Alone, he speaks in his own voice, telling us how he was 'proclaimed'—outlawed—and escaped by hiding in a hollow tree. His disguise will be to make himself unrecognizably base, assuming the look and manner of the 'Bedlam beggars'. These mad vagrants 'Strike in their numbed and mortifièd arms / Pins, wooden pricks, nails, sprigs of rosemary' (2.2.181–2). Edgar's arms are not numbed; he feels the pins, pricks, and nails.

To better grasp what it is to be *vulnerable* in vulnerable reading, read Edgar's soliloquy slowly enough to feel the words on the flesh—contempt, grime, nakedness, persecution.

> I will preserve myself, and am bethought
> To take the basest and most poorest shape
> That ever penury in contempt of man
> Brought near to beast: my face I'll grime with filth,
> Blanket my loins, elf all my hairs in knots,
> And with presented nakedness outface
> The winds and persecutions of the sky.   (2.2.172–8)

These words also summon thoughts of illness. In the moment after the confirmation of a diagnosis, people anticipate how illness and treatment will change them. They have to ask Edgar's question: what shape am I willing to endure to preserve myself, especially if effects of treatment bring more proximate pain than the disease itself? Nobody can know what 'winds and persecutions' will have to be outfaced and what living as 'presented nakedness' will feel like, but they must will themselves to accept the unknown.

The weight of Edgar's decision to live 'in contempt of man' is expressed by the Shakespearean scholar S. L. Goldberg: 'no one can really know how much of his own identity he can bear to risk.'[2] Vulnerability is the moment when that question—*how much of my identity can I bear to risk?*—is imposed by some imminent threat. Present loss shades into an uncertain future: *how much more will be taken from me?*

'Poor Tom!', Edgar both names himself and laments his plight. Then he accepts his new identity: 'That's something yet: Edgar I nothing am' (2.2.187). Edgar the fugitive *proclaiming himself* as nothing is how he answers Goldberg's question: he is willing to give up *all* his identity. As Edgar, he is nothing, that echoing word *nothing* recalling Cordelia's reply to Lear's demand and Lear's 'nothing will come of nothing'. Edgar's faith is that something can come of his becoming nothing: Poor Tom is 'something yet', and that may be the possibility of something else. In becoming Poor Tom, Edgar survives. His courage to accept the cost of that survival might offer solace in a possible future when I have to decide how much of my identity I can bear to risk.

The visual image of Poor Tom conveys much that the word *survivor* flattens. I have struggled for decades with the word *survivor*, finding it indispensable but deceptive. The word risks obscuring the scars that will remain from being Poor Tom. How the actor is made up to appear on stage is a crucial production decision: how mortified should Tom look? On stage, a real human body becomes Poor Tom. The actor Michael Pennington writes in his memoir of playing Lear how the actor playing Edgar/Tom got sick from repeatedly being cold and wet during Act III's storm scene. The filth and blood might be make-up, but a real body was naked, exposed. Edgar falls much lower than Cordelia, whose exile is to become Queen of France. His is to grime his face with filth and stick his arms with pins and nails.

'A great wheel runs down a hill…'

Now Lear faces how much he can give up, as the props of what we call *identity* are kicked away. Lear cannot yet believe what is happening when he arrives at Gloucester's castle to find his messenger Kent has been put in the stocks by Cornwall. The punishment was not unreasonable: Kent was brawling with Oswald, Goneril's servant (he of 'weary negligence'). 'They could not, would not do't: 'tis worse than murder / To do upon respect such violent outrage' (2.2.211–12), Lear says. The violent outrage he feels is not on Kent's behalf but for himself. Those who represent Lear are extensions of his person, and so Cornwall's act is 'worse than murder' *if* Lear is still the personification of the state, as its king. The political issue is who Lear is, after his partial abdication. The drama of vulnerability is the perpetual coming of the unimaginable: *They could not, would not.* Not only kings cling to beliefs about the limits of what *they*, whoever they are, 'could not, would not' do. Those beliefs mark the boundary of any person's sense of security. But then they, whoever *they* are, show they actually can, and will. The unimaginable is always there, possible, waiting. How much will they—or *it*—demand that I give up?

'Let go thy hold when a great wheel runs down a hill lest it break thy neck with following' (2.2.258–60), the Fool advises Kent while Cornwall and Regan further insult Lear by delaying their appearance. Their delay shows the wheel turning faster: the movement into chaos gathers speed, and before it stops necks will be broken. But no one is about to let go. Letting go is afforded no privilege in Lear's world, nor is letting go always possible in any world.

When letting go is not an option, what is left is fidelity. Maybe the Fool recognizes Kent; if anyone can see through disguises, he can. He recognizes enough to sing a song that expresses what he shares with Kent, foolish as that is.

> That sir which serves and seeks for gain,
> And follows but for form,
> Will pack when it begins to rain,
> And leave thee in the storm.
> But I will tarry, the fool will stay,
> And let the wise man fly:
> The knave turns fool that runs away,
> The fool no knave, perdy. (2.2.264–71)

In illness and other life crises, people will 'pack when it begins to rain, / And leave thee in the storm'. Singing the Fool's song can bring solace, in part by honouring those who do stay. The final word, perdy, is a slang variant of *par dieu*, by God, and it does more than make a rhyme: the Fool is pledging something, witnessed by Kent who is suffering for what he has pledged. The storm the song evokes is still a metaphor; when it becomes real, the Fool will not run away.

'O, reason not the need!'

More props of Lear's identity crumble when Cornwall and Regan finally deign to greet him and Goneril arrives. Lear realizes the sisters are allied. Their harmony has its high point in a kind of duet, bidding down the number of knights they will allow Lear to keep. Fifty becomes twenty-five, until finally Regan asks 'What need one?' (2.2.467). Lear confronts exactly how much of his identity he can bear to lose.

'O, reason not the need!' (2.2.468), Lear responds to his daughters' hectoring. His plea speaks for anyone holding on to who they have been. Lear knows that distinctly human need goes beyond practical utility: he reminds his daughters that their fine dresses scarcely keep them warm. He doesn't continue the argument, but it's clear enough: the dresses tell his daughters and those around them who they are, just as the presence of his knights reminds Lear and others who he is.

Finally Lear has only the gods to cry out to, as the sisters' demands reduce his claims to what has supported his dignity:

> You heavens, give me that patience, patience I need!
> You see me here, you gods, a poor old man,
> As full of grief as age, wretched in both.
> If it be you that stirs these daughters' hearts
> Against their father, fool me not so much
> To bear it tamely; touch me with noble anger. (2.2.475–80)

Old age equals grief, 'wretched in both'. Lear grieves himself: he who has been king. He prays for 'noble anger'. I need to be reminded that anger can be noble, because most of the anger we have seen, especially Lear's anger, is closer to petulance. The need to discriminate between angers will recur.

Lear deteriorates into pathos as he curses Goneril and Regan both:

> ... No, you unnatural hags.
> I will have such revenges on you both,
> That all the world shall—I will do such things—
> What they are yet I know not, but they shall be
> The terrors of the earth! (2.2.482–6)

In these words Lear is the shadow of himself that the Fool perceived earlier. 'What they are yet I know not' is the cry of a child frustrated in its powerlessness. Lear exits on the line: 'O fool, I shall go mad!' (2.2.489). He already seems half mad.

The sisters now seal who they will become. Goneril says Lear 'must needs taste his folly' (2.2.494). Regan repeats that she will still take in her father, but 'not one follower' (2.2.496), which is to say, she will house Lear as her father but not as a king. Her offer can be spoken with varying conviction. Gloucester sets the scene for the next Act:

> Alack, the night comes on, and the high winds
> Do sorely ruffle, for many miles about
> There's scarce a bush. (2.2.505–7)

These lines become a separate poem that I want to commit to memory, in part for the rhythm of the words, but more as they evoke vulnerability's imminent threat: the need to find shelter when there is none. Yet Gloucester speaks from a place still secure, and his words give the coming storm a dangerous enticement, a thrill that's seductive. I question how much comfort the lines will bring once the storm breaks, but they are something to say while we wait.

* * *

As the castle doors close on Act II, my reading goes back to Lear's plea, *O, reason not the need!* I think of that line often. It recalls conversations with my father when I have felt compelled to play a part that he might have likened to Goneril and Regan. In our lives, instead of 100 knights our longest standing difference was over a blue truck, a small urban sort of truck that my father bought more than thirty years earlier, a few years before he retired. He and my mother packed their vacation gear in that truck. The truck's two-seat cab marked their final stage of life as a couple, when their lives needed only those two seats.

The truck had a standard five-speed transmission, and over the years my father became especially dangerous pulling into traffic. He had no sense of there being a problem, but members of the family stopped wanting to be his passenger. Neighbours expressed concern. Then he put a dent in the side of the truck as he backed it out of the garage, and worse yet, he didn't notice. My wife happened to be there. He barely acknowledged the accident had happened.

Lear measures his identity in the size of his retinue. In our world, ceasing to drive is one of the significant thresholds when old age becomes incapacity; not only for men, it can be the singular threshold. It fell to me to persuade my father that he had to stop driving. Those were some of our worst conversations: there was none of Lear's cursing, but each of us was convinced the other could not understand what was at stake. The stakes for each of us were equally real.

Ultimately my father sold the truck to the owner of the garage up the street who had kept it running long after the younger mechanics had no idea how to work on such a vehicle. That man giving my father a token payment was an act of true generosity: he realized my father had to retain a sense of the truck's tangible value. That sale was the best possible ending. But I'll never forget my father, then nearly 100, pleading how he had always had a car, ever since he was an age he could scarcely remember. His other car sat in the garage for several years, uninsured with no battery, but a tangible affirmation of what could not be given up.

In the small scale of our less than tragic lives, we all have needs that cannot be reasoned. For me it's books. 'My train are men of choice and rarest parts' (1.4.235), Lear says of his knights, and that is how I regarded my books. Half my career was before the electronic retrieval of texts. Especially then, an academic life was marked by the accumulation of a library: books I once reviewed, taught, and based my own writing on; books I had been given by colleagues who had written them; and books I ought to have read but never did. Students and colleagues came to my office to borrow books. When I retired, my university library received many of my books, but I took as many home with me. I needed them as tangible representations that I was still a professor, with the tools of my trade to show it.

But once I took the books home, they became more a hoard than a circulating library. I have spent considerable time in the last few years finding homes for books I wish I'd given away when it was easier. Each donation is an admission to myself of inquiries I will not pursue. But each book donation is also a claim to what I do not need in order to be who I still am. Lear's tragedy of identity is being able to see only what he cannot be again. But writing that, I am haunted by the thought: maybe I'm just not that old, yet. When does the lightness of dispossession turn to pure loss?

'O, reason not the need!' We need whatever reminds us who we are, to sustain our fragile sense of what separates us from the abyss—our fear of *nothing*. Lear's pathos is being reduced to pleading his need. Edgar's heroism is his willingness to tolerate reducing himself to nothing, a condition of pure possibility, accepting whatever pain and baseness must be endured to sustain that possibility. It matters that Edgar is younger. Old age need not be 'full of grief' and wretched as Lear calls himself, but it carries the realization that gone is gone, lost is lost.

4

THE LOST, THE MAD, AND THE IMAGE OF HORROR

'Poor naked wretches.' (3.4.31)

Until now, the storm has been a metaphor.

Until now, Goneril and Regan have had some cause for their treatment of Lear.

Until now, Lear has been sheltered by at least a pretence of respect.

Until now, Edgar only foretold becoming Poor Tom, not knowing what being Poor Tom would do to him.

Until now, Cornwall has played the part of the reasonable lord.

Now the storm breaks.

'Where's the king?'

Shakespeare's language and storms call each other forth. In Gloucester's forecast at the end of Act II, the coming storm is a metaphor of unsheltered abandonment. The literal storm that now breaks retains the force of that metaphor. Identities become unhinged in a storm. 'Who's there?' Kent asks, and that question repeats throughout Act III. Kent is not sure who's there because the storm has separated Lear's party and the rain obscures vision, but the question cuts deeper. By now neither Lear nor Edgar could offer a sure response if either asked himself who's there. Kent recognizes who's there as a Gentleman loyal to Lear and asks where the king is. But the storm not only unhinges identities, it also fractures dialogue: characters answer each other aslant. The Gentleman responds by describing Lear in psychological space, not geographical location. His response deserves quotation partly for the pure pleasure of its words and images:

> Contending with the fretful elements;
> Bids the wind blow the earth into the sea
> Or swell the curlèd waters 'bove the main,
> That things might change or cease.   (3.1.4–7)

These lines ask to be memorized for future need, especially, 'That things might change or cease'. Lear is on one of life's downward slides when the only hope is that things might change or cease. In illness it's the vain hope that lab tests got mixed up: somebody else's pathology has got my name on it by mistake; I'm actually feeling better. But the downward spiral won't suddenly reverse; the storm must be faced.

'But who is with him?' (1.3.8), says Kent. The answer is the Fool 'who labours to out-jest / His heart-struck injuries' (3.1.9–10). On this heath in the storm, Lear's injuries are too heart struck to be out jested. Time runs out for the Fool.

'More sinned against than sinning'

Ranting against fate is one way to encounter vulnerability. Lear seeks to out-bellow his heart-struck injuries, which he personifies as the storm. 'Blow winds and crack your cheeks! Rage, blow' (3.2.1), begins the speech that impressed me as a teenager, when I first saw *King Lear*. Now, as a vulnerable reader, I prefer Lear's professions of humility: 'here I stand, your slave, / A poor, infirm, weak and despised old man / ... I will be the pattern of all patience: / I will say nothing' (3.2.19–20, 37–8). Whatever I would prefer, Lear goes back to shouting down the storm: 'Let the great gods / ... Find out their enemies now' (3.2.50, 52).

That speech ends with Lear's monumental, much quoted self-justification: 'I am a man / More sinned against than sinning' (3.2.60–1). *Is he?* That's the question for vulnerable reading, because life's troubles invite blaming something, either persons or personifications, whether these are storms or diseases. As we see Lear standing amid thunderbolts that do risk singeing his white head (3.2.6), it's easy to accept his self-description of being victim of his daughters' ambitions. When we stand amid whatever form thunderbolts take in our lives, it's easy to see ourselves assaulted.

Lear's claim is not without some truth, but it misguides. The classic Buddhist text, *The Dhammapada*, begins by pointing out the error of the soul that says, 'He abused me, attacked me, / Defeated me, robbed me!' 'For those carrying on like this,' the sage comments, 'Hatred does not end.'[1] Lear is caught in that cycle, as are Goneril and Regan.

The vicious destructiveness of Goneril and Regan is real, but Lear is no victim. I see him as someone whose sins instigate others to worse sinning, which includes sins against himself, fuelling his self-justifications that ignore how the cycle started. In *Henry IV, Part 2*, Sir John Falstaff describes himself: 'I am not only witty in myself, but the cause that wit is in other men' (1.2.6–7). Falstaff's wit brightly *instigates* the wit of others: it brings out wit that was latent in them. Goneril, Regan, and Cornwall do far worse damage than Lear does: he never tortures anyone or poisons his kin. On the contrary, Lear gives Kent time to gather resources for his exile and he sees the banished Cordelia well married. But Lear, loved as he is by his party, unleashes other characters' inner worst. Each's sins are tangled in the sins of others, further back than the play shows us. That's a family, or a kingdom. The question of *King Lear*, a question that deserves being called *great* among human concerns, is how to break the cycle.

'Man's nature cannot carry / Th'affliction'

To Lear's rants, Kent responds generously: 'man's nature cannot carry / Th'affliction nor the fear' (3.2.48–9). Lear represents every suffering soul for whom life out-storms what human nature can sustain. At that breaking point the question is no longer how much of the self someone is willing to give up in order to survive; Kent marks the line beyond which humans can ask no more of ourselves. What I call, always inadequately, *vulnerability* is the mixture of affliction and fear that Kent recognizes.

Led to a hovel where they can find shelter, Lear for the first time accommodates another's need. He comforts the Fool:

> My wits begin to turn.
> Come on, my boy: how dost, my boy? Art cold?

> I am cold myself.—Where is this straw, my fellow?
> The art of our necessities is strange,
> And can make vile things precious. Come, your hovel.—
> Poor fool and knave. I have one part in my heart
> That's sorry yet for thee.   (3.2.70–6)

If Lear's wits begin to turn, here they turn toward the humane. Lear puts himself on the same ground as his Fool: two bodies, both cold, a word that repeats. Lear knows he is no longer at court. Things that were once vile now seem precious; he and the Fool share their mutual necessity. Lear's wits will soon turn further, but for this moment humanity shines through assailed majesty.

In response to Lear's empathic gesture, the Fool sings his great song, a coda to Kent's line about affliction. In my imagined production of *King Lear*, the song would be repeated at the play's ending while the players slowly leave the stage. At this moment in the play, the song offers a soft counterpoint to the bellicose opening of 'Blow winds and crack your cheeks':

> He that has and a little tiny wit,
> With hey, ho, the wind and the rain,
> Must make content with his fortunes fit,
> Though the rain it raineth every day.   (3.2.77–80)

A risk of art is to force sadness into being beautiful, to aestheticize suffering. Yet we need works of art to do that: to enable finding beauty even outside a hovel in the wind and rain. The Fool does not exhort to bear up under affliction; when he sings, sadness shares its truth. *The rain it raineth every day.*

'the tempest in my mind'

In the storm where no one can be sure who's there, Lear deepens all that is uncertain by raising a subversive question, a question that deserves to be called modern for its refusal to accept what the established political order requires accepting. Who is anything—king or madman, noble or beggar, thief or justice—beyond what concentric circles of others both enable and demand that person to be? We are players, every one, cast in our parts, handed scripts and costumes, put on stage sets, directed in how to perform, and yet. For all that the self depends on props—Lear's hundred knights, his daughters' dresses—to ourselves we feel like more than the sum of what props us up. Selves may be performances, but performances require a performer. Does what we call an *authentic* self refer to a potential performer who is either realized or distorted in any performance—who's there? Who then gets to say whether any performance is an authentic realization of the inner performer or an inauthentic distortion? Being king is a performance that is extreme in the difficulty of stopping performing it. Edgar, in an immense act of will, becomes Poor Tom and performs madness—but once enacted, that madness is even more difficult to stop performing. King and beggar, two performances that drive their performers to madness, now meet.

Lear, invited by Kent to enter the hovel, turns cranky. 'Let me alone' (3.4.4), he replies. Kent asks again, and now Lear speaks what he feels: 'Will't break my heart?' he says, probably surprising Kent. Lear's next words suggest that as cold as the hovel's comfort is, even so little would be an unbearable contradiction to the shame and rage he feels. There is no taking shelter from all that has brought him to this place, both his sins and sins against him.

> Thou think'st 'tis much that this contentious storm
> Invades us to the skin so: 'tis to thee,
> But where the greater malady is fixed
> The lesser is scarcely felt...
> The body's delicate: the tempest in my mind
> Doth from my senses take all feeling else
> Save what beats there.   (3.4.8–16)

In Lear's speech, the body's delicacy is its sensitive responsiveness to what distresses it most, and what is that? Certainly, physical distress is real: the cold and rain that invade the skin. But Lear's foremost suffering is the tempest in his mind—memories, regrets, unanswered insults. Those render him not insensitive to the cold, but rather, I think, the cold is a kind of confirmation. He will not enter the hovel because his heart is already broken.

Those lines break my heart by what they make me remember. During prolonged illness the tempest in the mind can make the disease scarcely felt. Illness is one of the storms in which the props fall away and a person is left with 'what beats there', and not only what, but *who*? At some point in an illness each is left alone to confront our own 'greater malady'. Lear's tempest certainly includes continuing recrimination against his daughters. But I choose, with little basis in the text and at the risk of making Lear who I want him to be, to think the greater part of Lear's tempest is thoughts of what he himself has done to get where he is, whom he has wronged. The last words, 'what beats there', suggest the heart, and Lear's heart holds painful remembrance.

My reading is affected by the 1985 film adaptation *Ran*, directed by Akira Kurosawa, setting *King Lear* in medieval Japan with shifts in plot that disclose unseen aspects of the original. When the Lear character arrives at the hovel, he finds living there a dispossessed young nobleman, Tsurumaru. Once the king seized this man's lands and ordered him to be blinded. Tsurumaru embodies the king's history of violence, his crimes of power that are now rebounding on himself. The word *ran* means chaos. That chaos began long before the king abdicated, and his journey is across the landscape of his memory. The tempest in his mind is the life he now walks through, feeling its effects as much as seeing them.

Lear tells the Fool to enter the hovel first. 'I'll pray, and then I'll sleep,' he says (3.4.30). What follows truly is a prayer, Lear's testimonial plea for justice and human compassion:

> Poor naked wretches, wheresoe'er you are,
> That bide the pelting of this pitiless storm,
> How shall your houseless heads and unfed sides,
> Your lopped and windowed raggedness, defend you
> From seasons such as these? O, I have ta'en
> Too little care of this! (3.4.31–6)

I would like to attend a church that made these lines part of its liturgy; when some churches have included similar words, they have been marginalized for doing so. The storm that assails the poor naked wretches is again both a metaphor for all life's assaults on bodies and spirits, and it is the reality of present circumstance. The storm too easily blows through the 'windowed raggedness' that cannot shield bodies left to 'bide the pelting of this pitiless storm'. These words, like Edgar's 'To take the basest and most poorest shape' soliloquy, make vulnerability felt on the skin.

When I dare to imagine that I hear Shakespeare speaking through one of his characters, the 'Poor naked wretches' lines are what I would most like to think are Shakespeare's own prayer: 'defend you / From seasons such as these'.

'Fools and madmen'

Wretchedness more wretched still: the Fool comes out of the hovel, terrified by what he calls 'a spirit'. We now see Tom, which is to see what living this way has done to Edgar. Reading or performing *King Lear* poses the question of just how mad Edgar-as-Tom is. Edgar brings Tom into being; for a time it seems Tom takes over Edgar. But Tom will also bring into being whatever Edgar can become.

What follows is a demented, funny, and pity-inducing dialogue between Lear and the one he calls 'this philosopher' (3.4.144) 'Did'st thou give all to thy daughters? And art thou come to this?' (3.4.50–1), Lear asks. Tom is not wholly oblivious to Lear but speaks his own interior monologue: 'Who gives anything to poor Tom?' (3.4.52). He begins a refrain, 'Tom's a-cold!', that becomes the drone note that anchors whatever melody is played above it, calling us to remember what is at stake: the naked body. I ask myself whether these two have fallen to this fellowship of truth and madness, or have they risen to it? As always in Shakespeare, the answer is both, and another riddle for the vulnerable reader: What in rising falls, and in falling rises?

'This cold night will turn us all to fools and madmen' (3.4.77), says the Fool, who may be surprised to find himself the sanest person in the room. Among these fools and madmen, the vulnerable reader can feel strangely at home, in the fellowship of those who seem to have no further to fall. That fellow feeling is what Lear expressed earlier when he said to the Fool 'Art cold? / I am cold myself' (3.2.71–2): the sharing of afflictions too great to bear alone.

Lear now addresses the specific naked wretch before him, but here I question how he responds to vulnerability:

> Thou wert better in a grave than to answer with thy uncovered body this extremity of the skies. Is man no more than this? Consider him well. Thou ow'st the worm no silk, the beast no hide, the sheep no wool, the cat no perfume…Thou art the thing itself: unaccommodated man is no more but such a poor bare, forked animal as thou art.   (3.4.96–102)

What is 'the thing itself: unaccommodated man'? For me, Lear romanticizes wretchedness as an ideal of being able to live without accommodating anyone else. 'Off, off, you lendings! Come, unbutton here' (3.4.102–3), he then says. His clothes represent all that has been merely lent to Lear, and lent for reasons no more just than why Tom's clothes were taken away. Lear seeks to join Tom in the condition of owing nothing to persons or to beasts: nothing owed to the worm that produces silk, or to the sheep that grows wool, or to the cat that secretes what becomes perfume. Lear, who has demanded everyone else accommodate him, now imagines being unaccommodating as a condition of pure humanity. He rightly recognizes how much his life owes to others, but he then wants to believe he could live without incurring that debt. And still being Lear, he cannot cease to command: he orders others to unbutton him, paradoxically demanding others' accommodation to his fantasy of becoming unaccommodated. That fantasy enables Lear to evade the question of what he can give back for what he has received. If unaccommodated, then he is without obligation.

Kent's refrain 'Who's there' (3.4.119) now responds to Gloucester's entrance. Gloucester has the same doubt: 'What are you there? Your names?' (3.4.120). How existential these questions are is suggested by the answer that comes, aslant, from Tom, whom Gloucester should see is there but cannot recognize. Tom tells his father who Edgar now is:

> Poor Tom, that eats the swimming frog, the toad, the tadpole, the wall-newt and the water, that in the fury of his heart, when the foul fiend rages, eats cow-dung for salads, swallows the old rat and the ditch-dog, drinks the green mantle of the standing pool, who is whipped from tithing to tithing, and stocked, punished and imprisoned. (3.4.121–6)

Gloucester ignores his unrecognized son and asks Lear to enter the hovel. For me, Tom's words are the clearest evocation of how a poor naked wretch lives.

'The grief hath crazed my wits' (3.4.161), Gloucester says next. Grief has become an invisible actor on the stage, affecting each—Kent, Edgar-as-Tom, Lear, Gloucester—in his own way. This scene takes us as readers to the edge of having our own wits crazed. I seek less to interpret it than to be affected by it, letting myself become caught up in its swirl.

The final move in this dialogue of non sequiturs belongs to Tom, who takes over the Fool's role. He conflates what scholars guess was probably a line from a ballad with a fragment of a nursery rhyme, speaking both summary and prophecy:

> Child Rowland to the dark tower came,
> His word was still: fie, foh and fum,
> I smell the blood of a British man. (3.4.176–8)

'Child' is a candidate for knighthood, thus intimating a quest; is this how Edgar sees himself? The pronouns *his* and *I* are ambiguous as to whether Rowland, Edgar, or another speaks. But whoever's voice it is, Tom's right: the smell of blood is in the air.

'Leave him to my displeasure'

Lear in the storm was an image of vulnerability, but nothing happens to him like the horror that awaits Gloucester. To face this scene, two lines deserve to be reprised. First, Edmund's words to Edgar, describing a scene that never happened: 'I have told you what I have seen and heard, but faintly, nothing like the image and horror of it' (1.2.151–3). As often as I have read and seen this scene, I still hope Shakespeare will tell what follows faintly, but instead he compels us to witness the image and horror of it. Second, recalling Kent's 'man's nature cannot carry / Th'affliction nor the fear' (3.2.48–9), we now see how much affliction and fear can be carried.

'Hang him instantly,' says Regan (3.7.4), when they hear Gloucester has returned from aiding Lear. 'Pluck out his eyes,' says Goneril (3.7.5). It's not the first reference to eyes: back in Act I, when Lear felt betrayed by Goneril, he says: 'Old fond eyes, / Beweep this cause again, I'll pluck ye out / And cast you' (1.4.275–7). But however the threat is anticipated, I still wonder what elicits the full fury of the sisters. Gloucester has aligned himself with Lear and Cordelia, but he has done little; locking him up would fit his offences. I have to understand the sisters projecting onto Gloucester their pent-up rage at their father, whose curses on them they now repay. The sisters also need a common enemy at this moment when their rivalry over Edmund is beginning to unravel their alliance, tenuous as it always was. Joint violence momentarily unites them.

'Leave him to my displeasure' (3.7.6), Cornwall says. He dispatches Goneril to rally her troops and sends Edmund with her, because what Cornwall plans to do to Gloucester is 'not fit for your beholding' (3.7.8). Gloucester is brought in.

Cornwall and Regan interrogate Gloucester, but their questions are only foreplay to their sadism; they increase their excitement by delay. Gloucester admits he has sent the king to Dover, and Regan asks why there. He speaks his own fate: 'Because I would not see thy cruel nails / Pluck out his poor old eyes' (3.7.63–4). Gloucester rehearses the cruelties done to Lear, ending with a defiant prophecy: 'I shall see / The wingèd vengeance overtake such children' (3.7.72–3). 'See't shalt thou never' (3.7.74), Cornwall replies and gouges out one of Gloucester's eyes. Regan calls for him to maim the other, but they are interrupted by Cornwall's servant.

This unnamed servant commits the most singular act of moral courage in *King Lear*, saying:

> Hold your hand, my lord:
> I have served you ever since I was a child,
> But better service have I never done you
> Than now to bid you hold.   (3.7.80–3)

The servant calls on Cornwall to exercise authority worthy of service, rather than becoming the tyrant he makes himself by torturing Gloucester. His words recall Kent calling Lear to account when he banishes Cordelia: Kent never did Lear better service. Cornwall's servant knows his master will not treat him with Lear's restraint.

'All dark and comfortless,' says Gloucester (3.7.94), after Regan stabs the servant in the back and Cornwall finishes what he began. Gloucester's physical pain is intensified by the tempest in his mind when Regan tells him that Edmund informed them of Gloucester's alliance with Cordelia. Gloucester realizes he had it all wrong: Edgar was the faithful son, and Edmund betrayed them both. As Gloucester bears his affliction, I believe it counts for something that he had a witness in the servant who tried to stop Cornwall.

Gloucester's prophecy that vengeance would overtake Lear's children already begins to come true. 'Regan, I bleed apace: / Untimely comes this hurt' (3.7.108–9), Cornwall says, wounded while fighting the servant. Again a word or phrase encapsulates so much; here it's *untimely*. Is suffering always felt as untimely? I recall a woman in a discussion group I was leading in an extended care home—she seemed ancient to me then, though she was younger than my father is now. In what I intended as deference to age, I speculated that there might be a time of life when illness was no longer unexpected. 'You're always surprised,' she gently reminded me. Cornwall is not surprised for long.

Regan tells the servants to thrust Gloucester out 'and let him smell / His way to Dover' (3.7.103–4), to join Cordelia. I read about a stage production that had Cornwall fall and die unattended, Regan's interest having already moved on to Edmund; directors must decide. But whether or not Regan mourns Cornwall, I can't. His penultimate words match Regan for venom: 'Turn out that eyeless villain: throw this slave / Upon the dunghill' (3.7.107–8). If we had any doubt that we have descended into hell, we should now be certain of it.

5

RECONCILIATIONS

'No cause, no cause.' (4.6.80)

What can calm the tempest in the mind when that is suffering's greater part?
A pantomime on a clifftop, lucidity in madness.
What has been unravelling comes together. For a few moments, what always should have been truly is.
We smell mortality. We see grace enacted.

'And worse I may be yet...'

Vulnerability is felt: a tightness in stomach or chest, a weakness in legs or hands. Vulnerability happens in the suddenness of perceiving something amiss, liable to get worse; it's the feeling that life has changed irrevocably. But falling requires a place to fall from. Edgar evokes such a place in a speech setting himself beyond vulnerability. The storm is past. How Edgar separated from Lear's party is left for us to fill in; whatever has happened, he is alone and at his most content. He speaks what might be called his song of the road; it wants to be sung:

> Yet better thus, and known to be contemned,
> Than still contemned and flattered. To be worst,
> The lowest and most dejected thing of fortune,
> Stands still in esperance, lives not in fear:

> The lamentable change is from the best,
> The worst returns to laughter. Welcome, then,
> Thou unsubstantial air that I embrace!
> The wretch that thou hast blown unto the worst
> Owes nothing to thy blasts.   (4.1.1–9)

A vulnerable reader hears Edgar having retreated into lyricism that's flown from reality. He seems to believe he can play the role Lear cast him to be: unaccommodated man, owing nothing, needing only the air to live on. He believes he has survived becoming the 'most dejected thing of fortune' and he now 'lives not in fear', either the nobleman's fear that he is only being flattered, or anyone's fear of some 'lamentable change' in fortune. He stands in 'esperance', hope that what has been worst 'returns to laughter'. Someday he will look back on this and find it funny. His confidence that the worst is past is his vulnerability. Edgar has learned independence—and I don't want to diminish either the cost or the value of that. Now he learns mutual dependence.

While Edgar is proclaiming the joys of esperance, Gloucester enters, led by an Old Man. Seeing his mutilated father, Edgar plummets: 'World, world, O world!...thy strange mutations make us hate thee' (4.1.11–12). His youthful optimism turns to existential despair. But then Edgar hears what he most needs to hear, that his father knows he wronged him, and he is the centre of Gloucester's remaining hopes. Gloucester instructs the Old Man who guides him to be gone; it's dangerous to be aiding him. The Old Man protests, 'You cannot see your way.' Gloucester responds from the depths of regret:

> I have no way and therefore want no eyes:
> I stumbled when I saw...O dear son Edgar,

The food of thy abusèd father's wrath!
Might I but live to see thee in my touch,
I'd say I had eyes again!   (4.1.20–1, 23–6)

I stumbled when I saw is another line that belongs in a liturgy. Lear outside the hovel felt most keenly not the cold but the tempest in his mind; now Gloucester feels most the pain of having misrecognized Edgar. His present suffering is overtaken by his recognition of past mistakes. Gloucester's blindness, in all its pain, has a curious rightness for him: 'I have no way and therefore want no eyes'. Those words are spoken from a circle of misery lower than his son's earlier 'Edgar I nothing am' (2.2.187).

Edgar offers a coda to his father's despair, speaking lines to recall if we reach such a crisis. He is introduced by the refrain of uncertain identity, calling us to ask who this Edgar now is:

OLD MAN: How now? Who's there?
EDGAR: O gods! Who is't can say, 'I am the worst'?
    I am worse than e'er I was.
OLD MAN: 'Tis poor mad Tom.
EDGAR: And worse I may be yet: the worst is not
    So long as we can say 'This is the worst.' (4.1.27–32)

The worst is not so long as we can say 'This is the worst' is so complete in itself that the only way to be true to such words is, following Cordelia, to remain silent. Shakespeare, speaking through Edgar, acknowledges the limit to how far language can express suffering. For a while, being able to say 'the worst' can mitigate living that worst; language helps, even heals, and that's the point of vulnerable reading. But eventually comes a suffering that exceeds 'so long as we can say'. It awaits.

'When madmen lead the blind'

Gloucester can still say what is worst. The Old Man tells him that the person they've come upon is 'Madman and beggar too' (4.1.35). Gloucester sensibly questions how mad a man can be so long as he knows to beg; he then moves through regret to his bleakest vision of the human condition:

> He has some reason, else he could not beg.
> I'th'last night's storm I such a fellow saw,
> Which made me think a man a worm: my son
> Came then into my mind and yet my mind
> Was then scarce friends with him. I have heard more since.
> As flies to wanton boys are we to th' gods:
> They kill us for their sport.   (4.1.36–42)

Gloucester called on the gods to protect him when he was tied to the chair to be tortured. Now the gods have worse than vanished: they are in control but malign. The 'flies to wanton boys' metaphor is so quotably memorable that I might pass by *I have heard more since*. Those words remind me that humans are vulnerable not to malign gods, but to temporality: we live with provisional knowledge, having to act even though we always might learn more later. Edgar's moment of lyrical self-satisfaction in his 'lamentable change is from the best' speech ignored what *more* he would see. *I have heard more since* expresses the vulnerability of the present to what is not yet known.

"Tis the time's plague, when madmen lead the blind' (4.1.54), Gloucester says, affirming his wish to be left with Tom. He speaks literally, but taken as a metaphor, his words express finding ourselves enmeshed in a system that we need—our life may depend upon it—but that system seems at best out of anyone's control and at worst controlled by malign gods that torture for sport. Gloucester's words capture what we can feel about politics, about corporations, about hospitals, and about many families: everywhere the madmen lead the blind.

Edgar repeats for the final time his refrain, 'Poor Tom's a-cold', but now he adds an aside, telling us that he cannot stand to continue playing this part (4.1.60). So why, every commentator on *King Lear* asks, does Edgar not tell his father the truth of who he is? Why continue the charade that has outlived its original purpose of Edgar's escape?

The charade's new purpose begins when Gloucester tells Tom his cause in going to Dover:

> There is a cliff, whose high and bending head
> Looks fearfully in the confinèd deep:
> Bring me but to the very brim of it
> And I'll repair the misery thou dost bear
> With something rich about me: from that place
> I shall no leading need.   (4.1.76–81)

I shall no leading need haunts me as the ghost of some future possible eventuality; whether fearsome or welcoming, I cannot tell. 'I shall no leading need' is where vulnerability ends: the final solitude. Getting to that place is all Gloucester can imagine to be worth desiring. But he has the aid of someone who will lead him differently.

Edgar and his father's shared journey to the Dover cliff begins in their respective needs: Gloucester to end his misery that seems beyond repair, and Edgar to emerge from being Poor Tom. The time is not yet ripe for Edgar to tell his father the truth. Playing the part of Poor Tom is still inscribed on his flesh; it's no more a costume he can change out of than his father's blindness is a worst that will return to laughter. And I, reading, realize I need to be the silent third who also makes the journey to the cliff. I need to make that journey over and over, facing the part of me that needs to go there if I am to return to myself.

But *King Lear* is never only about individuals facing what they must to find themselves. Political concerns are the constant background. When Gloucester gives Edgar a purse as down-payment for his services, he makes explicit the message that Lear in his madness has already suggested: 'So distribution should undo excess, / And each man have enough' (4.1.73–4). Does Gloucester, or Shakespeare, believe that distribution of wealth is needed because of the erosion of what Gloucester, speaking to his retainer who guided him, has just called 'ancient love' (4.1.50)—the mutual obligations of feudal relationships in contrast to the contractual relations of the emerging economic order? The unravelling began when Lear spoke the language of that new economy by offering Cordelia 'a third more opulent' if she would enrich her declaration of love for him. Lear committed the double fallacy of equating love to its expression and making expression a commodity for exchange. Gloucester's call to undo excess begins to recognize this fallacy.

'His answer was, "The worse"'

Reading Shakespeare, no less than speaking him, is about breath and breathing. Breathing in, we reflect on what we read; breathing out, we let ourselves be carried along by the story's rush of events.

After a scene with so many lines to hold and ponder comes dialogue that gives us a moment to exhale. Readers can let ourselves be taken by the plot, just watching what happens.

Edmund leaves to prepare for battle, proclaiming to Goneril that he is 'Yours in the ranks of death' (4.2.26), prophetic for them both. Goneril replies in her most sexually explicit terms: 'To thee a woman's services are due: / My fool usurps my body' (4.2.29–30). That might be Shakespeare's nastiest entrance cue, but offstage, Albany has already expressed reciprocal feelings. Oswald has informed Goneril that Albany smiled on hearing the news that Cordelia's army had landed, and when told that his wife would soon arrive, 'His answer was "The worse"' (4.2.6). Albany enters.

Nobody writes a marital spat like Shakespeare. 'You are not worth the dust which the rude wind / Blows in your face' Albany tells Goneril. 'Milk-livered man' (4.2.34–6), she replies. Unfortunately for collectors of Shakespearean insults, news of Cornwall's death interrupts their creativity at expressing contempt. Albany's response makes his sympathies clear:

> This shows you are above,
> You justices, that these our nether crimes
> So speedily can venge. But, O, poor Gloucester!
> Lost he his other eye? (4.2.54–7)

Albany also learns from the messenger that Edmund informed against Gloucester.

And yet—here I breathe in, reflecting—when the final battle comes, Albany will align with Goneril, Regan, and Edmund. Why he chooses their side is another gap we must fill. Shakespeare's characters are as divided within themselves as any of us are.

'Patience and sorrow strove'

Cordelia returns, finally, to both the kingdom and the stage. But who's there, in this Cordelia? Vulnerable reading has a considerable stake in how she is presented, and Shakespeare wrote two different versions.

In the early 1608 Quarto version of *King Lear*, Cordelia's entrance is anticipated by a long dialogue between Kent and a Gentleman who has been attending her. 'You have seen / Sunshine and rain at once; her smiles and tears / Were like' (17.18–20) is typical of the Gentleman's descriptions of Cordelia. The Folio edition of 1623, published after Shakespeare's death, deletes that scene. It may be a matter of taste whether you like these lines, but liking isn't the issue. The lengthy Quarto descriptions turn *King Lear* toward being the tragedy of Saint Cordelia; the Gentleman's flowing praise, encouraged by Kent, is hagiography. Acted on stage, the words could be compelling. But is Cordelia there to be the character whom the Gentleman's words present her to be, a character that it's easy—too easy—to want her to be?

Making Cordelia a saint reduces other characters to her acolytes. When Kent—or the character who Kent becomes if this scene is included—hears the Gentleman's description of Cordelia's tears—'The holy water from her heavenly eyes' (17.31)—he appeals to planetary effects.

> It is the stars,
> The stars above us govern our conditions,
> Else one self mate and make could not beget
> Such different issues.   (17.33–6)

Such words when spoken by other characters diminish the speaker. Gloucester at his most gullible in Act I reasons the same way: 'These late eclipses in the sun and moon portend no good to us' (1.2.94–5). That sets up Edmund to be his most appealing when he calls such thinking 'the excellent foppery of the world' (1.2.108). Astrological influence aside, my problem is how Kent's speech asserts a binary contrast between Cordelia and her sisters: unqualified good versus unmitigated evil. Losing that opposition seems to me the best reason for the Folio editors cutting this scene.

What is wrong with sanctifying Cordelia as her sisters' polar opposite is expressed by the actor Eve Best, writing from her experience of having played both Beatrice and Lady Macbeth:

> It's immensely hard to create a defined black line around anybody. To say, beyond all reasonable doubt, *that* is the person ... They encompass, as we all do, an abundance of contrary qualities ... They have no end point.[1]

The Gentleman's overflowing praise of Cordelia draws that 'defined black line' around her: his words, reinforced by Kent's response to them, deny her contrary qualities. Defined lines, black or white, impede vulnerable reading. Living with vulnerability needs the flexibility of vision that Eve Best finds in Shakespeare: allowing 'an abundance of contrary qualities' in oneself and others. Learning to know characters as having 'no end point' prepares us for a world in which we may always hear more.

Watching the evolution of *King Lear* from the 1608 Quarto to the 1623 Folio reminds me that what we call *Shakespeare* is in motion, unfixed. Seeing changes between the two texts trains me to think of my life as a work of perpetual revision, undertaken in collaboration with my fellow actors, as we together write and rewrite the script of our lives. The Folio was published seven years after Shakespeare's death. I find solace in thinking of his work continuing to be written, or even better, of it continuing to write itself, his hand invisible but still moving. Shakespeare becomes not an historical figure but an ongoing dialogue.

*   *   *

Whether preceded by the Quarto's introductory build-up, or unheralded as in the Folio, Cordelia enters. She can be dressed in a gown or in battle fatigues. We readers choose how to imagine her; a director makes that choice for an audience. She asks how Lear might be restored to sanity, and the Doctor prescribes rest 'whose power / Will close the eye of anguish' (4.3.14–15), a bit of wisdom lost on modern hospitals. Is it possible, I wonder, to hear in this line one of Shakespeare's many puns on his name, Will? Is he encoding a claim or promise: Will will close the eye of anguish, his art will console and restore? As a vulnerable reader, I want to hear this pun.

Cordelia, who once left her motives opaque, now protests too much: 'O dear Father, / It is thy business that I go about' (4.3.25–6). 'No blown ambition doth our arms incite,' she ends the scene by affirming, 'But love, dear love, and our aged father's right' (4.3.29–30). She who rejected proclaiming love in return for a share more opulent now claims love's linkage to political *right*. What she would not say in words she will express in war.

'And more convenient is he for my hand'

King Lear affirms my observation that forces of evil are most often defeated because they self-destruct: what makes a cause evil also renders it unsustainable. We see that implosion as Oswald, Goneril's steward, delivers her letter to Regan; it's another moment to breathe out, enjoying the action's subtlety. Oswald seeks to withdraw, saying he must take another letter to Edmund, but Regan detains him. They go back and forth until Regan finally speaks in what can be called explicit euphemisms:

> My lord is dead: Edmund and I have talked,
> And more convenient is he for my hand
> Than for your lady's: you may gather more. (4.4.34–6)

I love these lines for what seeps out of their understatement: all that's implied in 'have talked' and 'more convenient', and Regan's closing 'you may gather more'. Oswald, knowing Goneril's plans with Edmund, gathers much more. Regan finally lets Oswald go, reminding him that he will be rewarded should he kill Gloucester.

If this short, edgy scene were cut in performance, audiences would not notice a gap in the plot. But the dialogue tightens the coils of the adversarial rivalry between Goneril and Regan. The scene also gives both the off-stage actors and the audience a moment to relax before three climactic moments.

'I took it for a man'

The madman leads the blind man toward the cliffs of Dover, where the blind man intends to jump. Edgar is no longer mad, but what he plans to act out is theatrical madness. As Gloucester and Edgar walk along, their dialogue could be a comedy sketch, were preceding events not so gruesome and the stakes of its outcome not so high. Gloucester believes they are climbing to the top of the Dover cliffs; Edgar works to sustain that illusion. They are, of course, on a level stage, but it's Shakespeare's stage, the stage where illusion becomes real if imagination makes it so. At this moment imagination doubles: one of the characters is imagining.

GLOUCESTER:	When shall I come to th'top of that same hill?
EDGAR (AS TOM):	You do climb up it now: look how we labour.
GLOUCESTER:	Methinks the ground is even.
EDGAR:	Horrible steep.
	Hark, do you hear the sea?
GLOUCESTER:	No, truly.
EDGAR:	Why, then, your other senses grow imperfect
	By your eyes' anguish.
GLOUCESTER:	So may it be, indeed. (4.5.1–9)

'How fearful / And dizzy 'tis to cast one's eyes so low ... The fishermen that walk upon the beach / Appear like mice ... I'll look no more, / Lest my brain turn' (4.5.15–16, 21–2, 26–7), Edgar says when their climbing ends, and hearing that, I feel vertigo. Gloucester gives his guide another purse and a jewel, says 'Bid me farewell' (4.5.37), and prepares to jump.

Edgar, speaking aside, questions his deception: 'Why I do trifle thus with his despair / Is done to cure it' (4.5.40–1). That expresses the dilemma of every nurse, doctor, family member, or care worker who colludes in a sick person's fantasy, encourages a half truth, and even says what is patently false, justifying that it's 'done to cure' or at least to minimize suffering. Edgar's verb, *trifle*, expresses the guilt in such acts. Edgar has good cause to hold his father guilty for what he has inflicted on him. Does Edgar suspect that he may be drawing out his father's misery for his own satisfaction? Acknowledging his motives may be mixed, Edgar has the honesty not to draw a line around himself within which he claims purity.

Gloucester renounces the world and blesses Edgar if he lives. The quality of the fantastic in what happens next is best expressed by the critic Jan Kott, who wrote the definitive Shakespeare book of the 1960s. Kott imagines this scene as a precursor to what was then known as theatre of the absurd:

> The blind Gloucester falls over on the empty stage. His suicidal leap is tragic. Gloucester has reached the depths of human misery; so has Edgar, who pretends to be mad Tom in order to save his father. But the pantomime performed by actors on the stage is grotesque, and has something of a circus about it. The blind Gloucester who has climbed a non-existent height and fallen over on flat boards, is a clown. A philosophical buffoonery of the sort found in modern theatre has been performed.[2]

After the jump, the visual pantomime turns into a dialogue that would otherwise be comic. Edgar adopts a new voice and persona as he revives Gloucester, who fainted when he fell. He perpetuates the illusion that Gloucester has jumped but somehow survived:

> Hadst thou been aught but gossamer, feathers, air—
> So many fathom down precipitating—
> Thou'dst shivered like an egg; but thou dost breathe. (4.5.59–61)

The comedy grows more grotesque when Gloucester asks whether or not he has really fallen. 'Look up a-height,' replies Edgar; 'do but look up' (4.5.68–9), setting up Gloucester's punchline: 'Alack, I have no eyes' (4.5.70). Did Elizabethan audiences laugh? Do we?

In a last twist, Edgar acts out another deception, saying to Gloucester:

EDGAR: This is above all strangeness.
            Upon the crown o'th'cliff what thing was that
            Which parted from you?

GLOUCESTER: A poor unfortunate beggar.
EDGAR: As I stood here below, methought his eyes
              Were two full moons: he had a thousand noses,
              Horns whelked and waved like the enragèd sea.
              It was some fiend…
GLOUCESTER: I do remember now: henceforth I'll bear
              Affliction till it do cry out itself
              'Enough, enough' and die. That thing you speak of,
              I took it for a man…(4.5.78–91)

Vulnerability, made visible at its extreme, unsettles what we take to be human. *I took it for a man* recalls Lear's line, seeing Poor Tom for the first time: 'such a poor, bare, forked animal as thou art' (3.4.101–2), and also Gloucester's earlier: 'I'th'last night's storm I such a fellow saw, / Which made me think a man a worm' (4.1.37–8). I have had such thoughts myself, once while passing through a cancer centre and seeing a man lying on a bed in a corridor. The unit was crowded with no room to offer him the dignity of privacy. No sheet or blanket covered him. His body was distorted by disease and pain; his eyes were open, but I couldn't tell whether he saw. I might then have said *I took it for a man*; cruel as that perception is, it was mine, and undeniable. If recalling Gloucester's words might have comforted me, I fear it would be my false hope to think such words could have comforted him, whose worst seemed beyond anything he could call the worst.

Edgar closes the scene with a stoic benediction to 'Bear free and patient thoughts' (4.5.93), which for me is far too pat, even dismissive, after what we have seen. Edgar spoke more truely when he called it 'above all strangeness': illusion and healing, tragic and comic, mixed. Kott's description seems to me unsurpassable: 'the precipice at Dover exists and does not exist. It is the abyss, waiting all the time. The abyss, into which one can jump, is everywhere.'[3]

For vulnerable readers, *King Lear* itself may be a precipice on which we must each respond to Gloucester's questions: What misery is best ended by whatever means? Who is this one who guides us? And following Kott's imagination of the scene, what grotesque pantomime do I find myself drawn into enacting? Who knows when they are playing the clown, and who can withstand that knowledge?

'It smells of mortality'

'But who comes here?' (4.5.93), Edgar says as Lear enters in torn clothes with a wreath of flowers on his head. Apparently he has slipped away from whomever attended him while Cordelia consulted with the Doctor. Yet when we see Lear in the next scene after this one, he is waking from the sleep prescribed by the Doctor, and it's as if this intervening scene never happened. For readers who are aware of this slippage, which a stage performance can smooth out, the meeting between Lear, Gloucester, and Edgar has a dream-like quality: the convergence of the three characters whose vulnerability is most immediate seems to occur outside of time.

Gloucester recognizes Lear's voice and asks if it is he. 'Ay, every inch a king,' Lear answers him. 'When I do stare, see how the subject quakes' (4.5.119–20). Or, once they did. *Every inch a king* recalls with intended irony the king we first saw disposing his lands, and it leads into Lear questioning what it is to be a king. He first mocks himself for believing the flattery of his courtiers, then denounces the pretensions of nobility. Lear speaks truth to his own previous power, but his speech soon spirals downward to his daughters' sins against him, finally descending to some of the play's most vicious misogyny: 'Down from the waist / They are centaurs, though women all above' (4.5.134–5) and worse from there. The violence of these words is tempered only if we ask ourselves whether Lear speaks in the voice of someone driven to madness or the voice of someone who has always thought this way. If the latter, we learn something about how Goneril and Regan got to be who they are. We go from Lear at his most egalitarian and sympathetic to Lear at his ugliest—Shakespeare forces us to accept these differences in one person.

Gloucester's 'O, let me kiss that hand!' (4.5.142) sets up a response that leads me to wonder what makes us call any lines great; what does *great* mean? Lear says of the hand Gloucester wishes to kiss:

Let me wipe it first: it smells of mortality. (4.5.143)

The words are too sane to be mad, yet they are tinged with madness if that is where the mind is driven by having been forced to recognize the unspeakable. Once again, Shakespeare's words evoke more than any meaning that can be specified, pointing beyond language.

Let me wipe it first, it smells of mortality. Deep in cancer and its treatment, I had to contend with people to whom my presence was obviously irreconcilable with the world they needed to wrap themselves in—the world I now wrap myself in. I represented mortality and mortality threatens—one person was honest enough to say so. 'Let me wipe it first…' expresses the alienation of those whose condition represents something intolerable not only to others but even to themselves. Hearing these words and being able to say them is a step toward making that alienation liveable—not yet the worst. Such words can offer themselves when something must be said but nothing else seems sayable. I hope I might never again need these words, but recognize that I likely will. How the words will come to mind, fitting that future occasion, will teach me more of what they can mean, but none of us ever exhaust that meaning, which continually points beyond.

Gloucester then reverses the 'Who's there?' refrain, asking Lear if he recognizes him. It's a poignant question, probing both how mad Lear has become and how unrecognizable Gloucester has been made to be. Lear deflects these issues with bad jokes about Gloucester's blindness, but then turns serious when he says: 'No eyes in your head…yet you see how this world goes' (4.5.154, 156). Gloucester responds with his memorable line: 'I see it feelingly' (4.5.157).

I see it feelingly is where Gloucester has been going: not to Dover but toward the second sight that a journey through suffering promises. 'I see it feelingly' plays counterpoint to Lear's 'every inch a king'. Kings cannot see feelingly; they are compelled to see through the lens of power and the necessity of maintaining it. But Lear, a king in rags with flowers in his hair, can speak of power feelingly, his next words astonishing in their overtly political message.

LEAR: What, art mad? A man may see how this world goes with no eyes. Look with thine ears, see how yond justice rails upon yond simple thief. Hark, in thine ear: change places, and handy-dandy, which is the justice, which is the thief? Thou hast seen a farmer's dog bark at a beggar?

GLOUCESTER: Ay, sir.

LEAR: And the creature run from the cur? There thou mightst behold the great image of authority: a dog's obeyed in office. (4.5.158–66)

Lear continues, now speaking in verse: 'Through tattered clothes great vices do appear: / Robes and furred gowns hide all' (4.5.171–2). Here is power, seen feelingly.

The great image of authority was chosen by the critic and scholar Harold Bloom as the title for his book about the character of Lear. In twenty-five lines, Lear goes from misogyny that I don't want to quote to the bluntest truth telling about power that none of us should forget. His metaphor of the cur describes the malicious side of authority, dependent on the ability to bite, concealed under robes of office. Such authority is the opposite of what Kent, seeking employment in disguise as Caius, claimed to see in Lear's face. Kent's version of authority—authority earned—remembers that it stands at risk of becoming what Lear now proclaims. True authority tolerates the self-doubt that the justice and the thief are separated only by who wears which costume: the tattered clothes through which vices appear, or the robe that hides all.

Shakespeare backs off immediately, having Edgar apologize: 'O, matter and impertinency mixed! Reason in madness' (4.5.181). By claiming Lear's words are double voiced—matter and madness, both—Shakespeare makes the speech acceptable. This book is not about the historical context of *King Lear*, but to hear the force of what Lear says—what Shakespeare is saying—remember that the play was written around 1606, during the early years of the reign of King James I. The Stuarts were committed to the divine right of kings: they considered themselves to be God's anointed rulers. That claim had become more explicit by 1623, when the first Folio was published. In 1606 it is beyond what Edgar calls impertinency to call authority a great image, a show depending on robes and gowns; to acknowledge that power rests on the ability of the dog to bite. James was patron to Shakespeare's acting company, the King's Men. They wore the king's livery. When *King Lear* was performed at court, if these lines were included, what did James hear in Lear's speech about the great image of authority? What did he make of the metaphor of a dog in office? We'll never know. But this scene makes me regard the survival of the play as a miracle.

'I know thee well enough,' Lear finally admits; 'thy name is Gloucester' (4.5.183). His next words should be condolences for the destruction he sees in Gloucester's face. *Did you suffer all this in my cause?* is what Lear ought to say. The words he does speak are eloquent, but he's being evasive.

> Thou must be patient; we came crying hither.
> Thou know'st the first time we smell the air
> We wail and cry. I will preach to thee: mark.   (4.5.184–6)

The words by themselves, out of context, are a moving evocation of the human plight. But in context, Lear displaces his responsibility onto the human condition. He conveniently forgets how his own actions set in motion the events leading to Gloucester's blinding.

Lear speaks two lines of memorable clarity, and then his complex metaphor veers into another revenge fantasy:

> When we are born, we cry that we are come
> To this great stage of fools. This a good block:
> It were a delicate stratagem to shoe
> A troop of horse with felt: I'll put't in proof,

> And when I have stol'n upon these son-in-laws,
> Then kill, kill, kill, kill, kill, kill!   (4.5.188–93)

The *great stage of fools* could be an alternative title for this book. In this context, I find Lear's cynicism comforting, without bitterness, even forgiving. It pairs with Gloucester's 'I have heard more since', expressing human limitation. I breathe out on hearing it said out loud that we live upon the great stage of fools. The words give me the patience that Lear says life demands; they enable me to see both my fellow fools and myself more feelingly.

In the 'delicate stratagem' of muffling horses' hooves with felt in order to sneak up on an enemy, which for Lear is now his daughters, I can't resist hearing Shakespeare telling us his authorial strategy in how he writes Lear's sermon on authority. Putting impertinent words in the mouth of a madman muffles a truth that otherwise would alert the enemy. Those who are represented in the figure of the beggar set upon by the cur must employ delicate stratagems.

Such talk has gone as far as it can go; amazing that it went so far.

'the art of known and feeling sorrows'

Lear departs and Gloucester shows that he is seeing feelingly. He finally asks Edgar what he should have asked long ago: 'what are you?' Edgar's reply transforms suffering into a hope of becoming more compassionate:

> A most poor man, made tame to fortune's blows.
> Who, by the art of known and feeling sorrows,
> Am pregnant to good pity.   (4.5.233–5)

I have heard many people describe themselves in similar terms as they reflect upon their recent experience of serious illness: by having felt sorrows, they claim to have gained a capacity for pitying others; they feel more fully human. Physicians who write about their own illnesses give compelling testimony to their increased empathy for their patients as a result of having themselves been 'made tame to fortune's blows'.

Edgar still does not tell his father who he is, but he offers him his hand, to lead him to safety before the coming battle. Gloucester blesses him. The blessing goes by quickly, but it is one of the play's two great reconciliations, a moment when we feel all can be well.

Violent irony then intrudes in the person of Oswald, who sees his chance to kill Gloucester. Edgar kills him, and in an almost comic move, the dying Oswald naively asks him to deliver to Edmund the letter in which Goneril plots to kill Albany after the battle. Albany was right that the gods are just: the false brother caused trouble with a forged letter; the true brother will now use a real letter to repair the damage. Lear rightly called it the stage of fools.

'Upon a wheel of fire'

'How fares your majesty?' Cordelia asks, as Lear awakes (4.6.44). He replies:

> You do me wrong to take me out o'th' grave:
> Thou art a soul in bliss, but I am bound
> Upon a wheel of fire, that mine own tears
> Do scald like molten lead. (4.6.45–8)

The Wheel of Fire is the title of a book by G. Wilson Knight that exemplified Shakespeare criticism in the 1930s. The metaphor stretches language to its limit, expressing what could not be said otherwise. Lear seems at the bottom of the abyss, until we recall Edgar's admonition: 'the worst is not / So long as we can say "This is the worst"' (4.1.31–2). Lear can still say.

Cordelia asks if Lear knows her, and we might think, has he ever? He answers: 'You are a spirit, I know: where did you die?' (4.6.50). Lear then gives a speech of awakening, or more accurately, rebirth:

> Where have I been? Where am I? Fair daylight?
> I am mightily abused. I should ev'n die with pity
> To see another thus. I know not what to say.
> I will not swear these are my hands. Let's see:
> I feel this pinprick. Would I were assured
> Of my condition! (4.6.53–8)

A change in Lear is marked by his words: 'I should ev'n die with pity / To see another thus.' Here is the plainest expression of empathy: the potential self-pity of 'I am mightily abused' converts into Lear imagining another person in his condition and feeling pity for that other.

Cordelia, drawing Lear to her, restores their relationship to what it always should have been:

> O, look upon me, sir,
> And hold your hand in benediction o'er me:
> You must not kneel. (4.6.59–61)

Lear responds: 'Pray, do not mock me', describing himself as a foolish old man and specifying his age, 'Fourscore and upward' (4.6.63–4). He also admits 'I fear I am not in my perfect mind'. Tentatively, Lear recognizes Kent and Cordelia. 'And so I am, I am' (4.6.74), she confirms when he asks if she is his daughter. But is she the same Cordelia who, not that long before, refused to speak of her love? Or is she who says 'I am' as changed as her father, so differently they now speak to each other?

The exchange that follows is for me, at least while I am hearing it, the most moving in all of Shakespeare:

> LEAR: Be your tears wet? Yes, faith. I pray, weep not:
> If you have poison for me, I will drink it.
> I know you do not love me, for your sisters
> Have, as I do remember, done me wrong:
> You have some cause, they have not.
> CORDELIA: No cause, no cause. (4.6.75–80)

Weep not, Lear says, but I do. My measure of any performance of *King Lear* is whether, by Cordelia's line, I find myself in tears. Cordelia has only 3 per cent of the lines in the play, but the emotional weight of *King Lear* depends on how much we have been brought to be able to hear in 'No cause'. Cordelia's ideal of what it means to be true has changed. She has every cause, in the sense of reasons to feel wronged. She is as the Gentleman has described her: 'the queen on special cause' (4.5.224), referring to her cause of restoring Lear to his throne. But at this moment of reconciliation, past wrongs and present political cause are moot. The world is reduced to parent and child, and the forgiveness that passes between them. Cordelia now speaks with a more profound understanding of truth than when she refused to speak before Lear's court.

Cordelia's 'No cause' expresses how I understand *grace*. Earlier, the Gentleman's hagiography included describing Cordelia as a Christ figure 'Who redeems nature from the general curse' (4.5.212). Now we see Cordelia perform the redemption of her father and also herself. She redeems not from any 'general curse' of Christian theology, but from Lear's specific curses, as these continue to reverberate on both their family and the kingdom. Cordelia's words are an act of grace because Lear has done nothing to earn them. She is still a character around whom no line can be drawn, and I still believe that part of her cause is with her sisters. But in this moment, she makes herself the 'soul in bliss' that Lear first takes her to be: the bliss of being able to seek her father's benediction, as she offers her forgiveness to him.

The Doctor pronounces a coda to the tableau of father and daughter that we should, if reading, allow ourselves to stop and hold as an image: 'the great rage, / You see, is killed in him' (4.6.84–5). Events will prove the Doctor's judgment premature. Lear's rage is quieted, not killed. But let us linger while we can on this enactment of grace.

6

LIVING WITH AN
UNPROMISED END

'Never, never, never, never, never!' (5.3.326)

The darker purpose unfolds its final vengeances.
One child is restored, another dies a senseless death.
What can promise us any ending?

'the chance of anger'

The battle between Cordelia's army and the forces of Goneril, Albany, and Regan happens off stage, with only its outcome reported; a reader could be excused for missing it. Yet Cordelia's defeat would have been a surprise, even a shock to audiences who expected the ending of *King Leir*, a play of unknown authorship that had been performed in London in 1594. Cordelia's victorious restoration of Leir at the end of that play followed the still older version told in Geoffrey of Monmouth's mythical history of Britain written around 1136 and known in a version published in 1585.[1] No less than in 1606, we today ask why Shakespeare changes the ending to have Cordelia lose the battle and then be assassinated in prison. He shows not triumphal succession, but vulnerability. He confronts us with a world in which being right does not entitle winning.

I approach Shakespeare's chosen ending by recalling a line that goes by quickly but for me could be an epigraph for the entire play. As Cornwall draws to fight the servant who tries to stop the torture of Gloucester, the servant defiantly responds: 'come on, and take the chance of anger' (3.7.88). Along with showing variations on authority and love, *King Lear* shows gradations of anger. Characters are as vulnerable to their own anger as to the anger of others: Lear takes the chance of venting his anger at Cordelia and Kent, setting chaos loose; Gloucester allows his anger against Edgar to crowd out cautious reflection on Edmund's motives. Kent, in disguise as Caius, when questioned by Cornwall why he attacks the disrespectful Oswald at Gloucester's castle, claims 'but anger hath a privilege' (2.2.62). That sounds like a good justification coming from Kent, whose selfless fidelity and willingness to speak the truth contextualize his aggressive masculinity. We enjoy seeing Kent attack the craven Oswald. But we should remember Lear's angry proclamation to Kent, 'Come not between the dragon and his wrath' (1.1.123), when Lear claims his anger grants the privilege of not listening to Kent's appeal. The acceptance that 'anger hath a privilege' is double edged, quickly turning against those who use it.

In the world of *King Lear*, anger has a legitimate place. Lear asks the gods to touch him with 'noble anger' (2.2.480). For me he shows noble anger in his indignation at people being reduced to the condition of poor naked wretches. Noble anger does not claim a privilege for itself; rather it takes the side of the oppressed, supporting their cause. Cornwall's servant's anger is noblest of all, self-sacrificing in its struggle to save Gloucester. *King Lear* calls upon us to learn the difference between self-justifying anger and anger on behalf of others. That distinction is risky: personal resentment readily conceals itself as righteous indignation.

Cordelia especially, but also Kent, walks a fine line between those differences of anger. Cornwall's anger is only rage that seems an end in itself; it lacks any nobility of purpose.

But whether self-justifying or noble, anger inevitably *takes a chance*; the servant expresses that clearly. When chance does not favour Cornwall, our moral world seems in order, operating as it should. But Cordelia's defeat in battle requires us to recognize the extent of human vulnerability to chance. Chance has no sense of fairness; it does not promise an ending that affirms what we believe is deserved. Shakespeare's chosen ending asks us whether, and how, we can live in such a world of vulnerability to chance.

'To the forfended place'

Bodies pile up in Act V. But Shakespeare anticipates the carnage with—least expected—comedy. This particular comedy may be better described by Jan Kott's preferred term, the grotesque. One of the ways that *King Lear* helps is by showing how laughter can be a form of witness that does not deny suffering, but rather sees it whole. In Act IV, characters we pity and hope for, Gloucester and Edgar, acted out the grotesque as they climbed the flat stage to the cliff top in Dover. Now the villains perform the grotesque. The deeper they sink in villainy, the funnier they become. Vulnerable reading learns to laugh darkly.

The comic performance begins when Regan asks Edmund if he loves Goneril. He replies with tactful evasion: 'In honoured love' (5.1.11). She asks more explicitly, employing a strange euphemism: 'But have you never found my brother's way / To the forfended place?' (5.1.12–13). To *forfend* is to forbid, and *forfended* means forbidden. Edmund denies he has, and whether he has his fingers crossed behind his back, we never know. We also don't know if he's stifling a laugh at Regan's choice of words, and whether we should be laughing: never has such a direct question been phrased so indirectly. Edmund is saved from further questions by Goneril arriving with Albany. The comedy continues as neither sister wants the other to be alone with Edmund, so the three exit together, leaving Albany on stage, odd man out.

Edgar then performs some serious plot business but with comic staging. Disguised as a peasant, he enters and gives Albany Goneril's letter, in which she conspires with Edmund to kill Albany after the battle. To prove the truth of the letter in trial by combat, Edgar says he will 'produce a champion' (5.1.38) after the battle. He exits just before Edmund, who likely would recognize him, enters; it's the comic style of a character who wants to avoid being seen getting off stage just in time. Edmund then makes the comedy explicit in his last soliloquy.

'To both these sisters have I sworn my love' (5.1.52), Edmund says, aware that he is playing the part of the lover caught between two women he has led on and making his delight in that role contagious. He considers his options; *jealous* here means suspicious, mistrustful:

> Each jealous of the other, as the stung
> Are of the adder. Which of them shall I take?
> Both? One? Or neither? Neither can be enjoyed
> If both remain alive.   (5.1.53–6)

Edmund's sociopathic charm evaporates as he realizes that to survive, not only Goneril and Regan must die. He plans to kill

Cordelia and Lear rather than adhere to Albany's intention to grant them mercy.

'men must endure . . .'

While the battle takes place off stage, I consider the futility of the fighting that all the characters accept without question. Cordelia has a kingdom at home in France, and she has Lear in her camp. She could have retreated, negotiating with Albany. Choosing to fight is her moment of taking 'the chance of anger' (3.7.88). But thinking of retreat is rationally strategic, weighing possible gain against risk, and that is not what tragic heroes do. The tragic hero's compulsion is to risk all; that both attracts and terrifies us. We feel small in the compromises we make, but we also feel relieved; our willingness to compromise keeps us alive.

Cordelia is every inch Lear's daughter: fighting is her 'long engrafted condition' (1.1.312). Cordelia's will to fight is neither a failing nor a virtue; it's her necessity. The battle has its own necessity as the outcome of all that has come before. Tragedy shows how necessity and futility blend. Destruction seems inevitable, yet is also utter waste.

'A man may rot even here' (5.2.9), Gloucester says when he hears Edgar's news that the battle is lost and Lear and Cordelia are prisoners. Edgar urges his father to get away, but Gloucester will go no further. Edgar has to play the caregiver who struggles to give the exhausted patient or loved one the will to go on. His exhortation begins with a line I wish he hadn't said, but then the short speech redeems itself:

> What, in ill thoughts again? Men must endure
> Their going hence, even as their coming hither:
> Ripeness is all: come on.   (5.2.10–12)

Against the assumption behind Edgar's opening rebuke, I believe in the value of 'ill thoughts'. Or to put it negatively, I believe in the damage that results from repressing thoughts that accurately assess an ill situation. But then Edgar's tone changes. 'Men must endure' affirms the validity of Gloucester's ill thoughts, but asks him to consider whether this is the moment to stop and rot here, or if further endurance might be possible. Edgar's 'Ripeness is all' is a variation of Hamlet's 'The readiness is all' (*Hamlet*, 5.2.152). Both lines precede the speaker engaging in a duel, and both invite multiple understandings. But each character's words lead in different directions. Hamlet ends his speech saying: 'Let be'. Edgar ends with 'come on'. Hamlet's readiness is an acceptance of whatever comes. Edgar is alert to whatever initiative the time is ripe for; he is not about to let be. Gloucester catches that spirit and assents to remain curious about what may yet be.

'And tell old tales . . .'

Cordelia's final speech, as she is sent to prison, begins in stoic resignation, then claims her own nobility of purpose, and ends with a question that becomes my most significant clue to what this daughter, princess, sister, queen of twists and turns *seeks*.

> We are not the first
> Who with best meaning have incurred the worst.
> For thee, oppressèd king, I am cast down:

Myself could else out-frown false fortune's frown.
Shall we not see these daughters and these sisters? (5.3.4–8)

The first two lines form another aphorism, well remembered: humans attempt, but their striving risks incurring the worst; that's life. Cordelia has risked for her father, and her regrets are for him alone. Then her concern turns sharply. Cordelia's last words in the play are about her sisters. I hear a tone of desperation, almost a plea, in 'Shall we not see these daughters and these sisters?' What does Cordelia want? Tragedy happens when one character's desire for acknowledgement encounters another's misrecognition. Cordelia wants to set right what Lear mistook in the first scene, when he valued the older sisters' false flattery over her true silence. She wants her sisters to witness her being led off to prison. She imagines that would force them to acknowledge her as the daughter so faithful that she is willing to be 'cast down' for the sake of the father whom they have oppressed.

The tempest in Cordelia's mind, more painful than losing the battle, is being denied the moment that reveals the truth of the family—who loves whom. She does not know that her sisters are already enacting their own final scene, with little thought for either her or Lear. Cordelia expends her last words asking for them, but they have forgotten her.

Lear responds to Cordelia with a string of negatives—'No, no, no, no' (5.3.9). He doesn't want to see Regan and Goneril. They merge among other players on the great stage of fools that he wants only to watch at a distance; he no longer has any stake in that game. We can scarcely elaborate all Lear implicitly says no to, starting with himself as he has lived, possibly extending to the gods. But Lear can still imagine life beyond *no*: he creates a fantasy of prison being what he once called Cordelia's 'kind nursery' (1.1.125) where he hoped to spend his last days. His speech is lyrical in its poetry, and beyond sadness in its naïveté:

> No, no, no, no! Come, let's away to prison.
> We two alone will sing like birds i'th'cage:
> When thou dost ask me blessing, I'll kneel down
> And ask of thee forgiveness: so we'll live,
> And pray, and sing, and tell old tales, and laugh
> At gilded butterflies, and hear poor rogues
> Talk of court news, and we'll talk with them too—
> Who loses and who wins, who's in, who's out—
> And take upon's the mystery of things,
> As if we were God's spies: and we'll wear out
> In a walled prison packs and sects of great ones
> That ebb and flow by th' moon.   (5.3.9–20)

Lear dreams of existing only in Cordelia's eyes and she in his. I wonder whether Cordelia finds her father's fantasy as enticing as he does, or if she gives any thought to the other king who is her husband. For me, Lear's fantasy expresses better than any of Shakespeare's often quoted love sonnets what two can be for each other, in mutual blessing and forgiveness, praying and singing, and telling old tales. I want to believe in that dream myself.

Edmund sends them away, giving the captain a note of instruction that we know orders their execution.

'The wheel is come full circle'

The last gasp of comedy begins when Regan proclaims her intention to marry Edmund. That sets up Albany's punchline, telling

Regan that his wife Goneril 'is bespoke' to Edmund already. Goneril, showing herself too intelligent for the part she is cast to play, comments: 'An interlude!' (5.3.93), meaning a comedy, not an intermission.

The speed of events then crowds out reflection. Albany orders a trumpet that summons Edgar, the anonymous challenger. Regan says she's sick, prompting Goneril's aside: 'If not, I'll ne'er trust medicine' (5.3.101), which is funny until we remember one sister is poisoning another. The comedy is over, and that is fatal for Edmund. He accepts the challenge, choosing to act the nobleman rather than sticking to being a trickster: 'What safe and nicely I might well delay / By rule of knighthood, I disdain and spurn' (5.3.153–4). He takes the chance of fighting. He loses. Goneril goes out every inch a king's daughter. Confronting Albany's proof of her plotting, her last words express how tyrants ever claim their right: 'the laws are mine, not thine' (5.3.169). But she knows the game is up and rushes off stage.

Edmund confesses, invoking the wheel metaphor:

> Th'hast spoken right: 'tis true,
> The wheel is come full circle: I am here.   (5.3.187–8)

Shakespeare is a moral pragmatist: he observes effects. The wheel has come full circle, and neither gods, nor planets, nor even fortune have turned it. I credit Edmund, who once derided Gloucester's foppery in blaming events on the stars, with accepting that his own acts have laid him low. Once again, we are never able to draw a black line around anyone. *I am here* is one of the play's most self-reflective lines. But it is spoken by one of the most self-absorbed characters: when a Gentleman brings news that Goneril has killed herself after confessing to poisoning Regan, Edmund turns their deaths into his own memorial.

> Yet Edmund was beloved:
> The one the other poisoned for my sake
> And after slew herself.   (5.3.245–7)

Edmund is a variation on how consuming the desire to be loved can be; his motives seem a twisted inversion of Cordelia's need to show how much she loves her father and deserves his love. He partially redeems himself by remembering to tell that he has ordered Cordelia's execution.

Among the deaths that follow each other quickly, Gloucester's alone gives me an ending I want and need. Edgar now seems to regret his delay revealing his identity to his father; thus care often has second thoughts, especially about what was not done.

> Met I my father . . . became his guide,
> Led him, begged for him, saved him from despair,
> Never—O, fault!—revealed myself unto him
> Until some half-hour past, when I was armed.
> Not sure, though hoping, of this good success,
> I asked his blessing, and from first to last
> Told him our pilgrimage: but his flawed heart—
> Alack, too weak the conflict to support—
> 'Twixt two extremes of passion, joy and grief,
> Burst smilingly.   (5.3.204–14)

To die with his heart 'Burst smilingly' counts as a good death. Gloucester has had the most horrific physical violence inflicted on him; among the deaths, he more than anyone dies as we hope for him.

Kent arrives, asking for Lear. His lines, 'I am come / To bid my king and master aye goodnight: / Is he not here?' (5.3.238–40) affect me as some of the saddest in a play filled with sadness. Kent assumes Lear is safe with Albany and all is well. He expects something so ordinary—to offer Lear a wish for his sound sleep— not knowing what we know enough to fear. The brevity of *Is he not here?* expresses grief so quietly. Repeating that question to myself, I recollect past losses and have forebodings of those in the future.

'Is this the promised end?'

I wrote earlier that for me stage productions of *King Lear* succeed or not when Cordelia replies 'No cause, no cause' to her father, as he asks her forgiveness. Our belief in that moment—our belief that there can be such reconciliation, such a togetherness of human spirits—takes us to a height of what we wish is possible: how high we go determines how far we feel ourselves falling now, when we see Lear enter with Cordelia's dead body. Reading stops; we need to form an image, to see that entrance. Then reading must also hear. Lear's grief begins with an animal cry that turns to desperate hope:

> Howl, howl, howl! O, you are men of stones:
> Had I your tongues and eyes, I'd use them so
> That heaven's vault should crack. She's gone for ever!
> I know when one is dead and when one lives:
> She's dead as earth. Lend me a looking-glass:
> If that her breath will mist or stain the stone,
> Why, then she lives.   (5.3.265–71)

Lear's *howl* responds to the worst that is beyond saying. Shakespeare has pushed language to its limits; now we hear wordless evocation. When Lear returns to words, he is able to speak only in conditionals, of what might be said: if we who watch as if we were stone were able to speak, what we might say would crack heaven's vault. Able to speak no further, Lear retreats into the delusion that Cordelia might live.

The three who witness the death that is and the death about to be respond as a chorus:

KENT: Is this the promised end?
EDGAR: Or image of that horror?
ALBANY: Fall and cease! (5.3.272–4)

Kent's words can be heard on two levels. Within the action of the play, Kent expresses his own stunned disbelief that instead of restoring Lear, he must confront Cordelia's death. As Kent is also heard within the theatrical space, he speaks for those in the audience who expected the old story of King Leir; Cordelia's death is not the triumphal ending they thought was promised. On both levels, the answer to Kent's question is *no*: this ending is neither what we believed this story promised, nor what we need to believe life promises. We felt promised an ending that would enable us to go on living in a world that includes so many images of horror. When the ending denies that promise, how do we continue living with its emptiness? Cordelia dies not to redeem our sins, but to question our lives.

Is this the promised end? Shakespeare tells the story as he does to make that question inescapable—can humans live without believing there is a promised end? Believing in a promised end depends on what it is that humans imagine is able to promise them justice, or love, or redemption. Gods are often imagined as promising something to humans, usually in exchange for what humans do to earn the gods' favour: right conduct, worship, forms of sacrifice. Kent and Cordelia have been faithful. The ending Kent now confronts is not what his faithfulness or hers deserved. If *this* is the end that happens, then there seem to be no promises.

Edgar speaks for us when he calls it the 'image of that horror'. The words echo Edmund telling Edgar that he conveyed 'nothing like the image and horror' (1.2.152–3) of Gloucester's hostility. Then, Edmund counterfeited, to use the word Shakespeare often prefers. Now, Edgar says what we see. A parent carrying the body of their dead child is an image emblematic of all human horrors. The particular horror of Cordelia's death is its uselessness: she is the victim of those who are already dead. Tragedy is an image of a horror that is simultaneously inevitable and truly, brutally without cause.

Albany's 'Fall and cease!' is a cry to the heavens that matches Lear's *howl*. Albany's words plead for an end to the intolerable: make it stop. *Fall and cease* is the last we can say when we confront the worst, when we see the world utterly fallen.

'Break, heart, I prithee, break'

But it does not yet cease. Lear's final, exhausted curses fall on those around him, whom he imagines interrupted him when he was about to revive Cordelia. His penultimate speech begins and ends with expressions of violence, his eulogy to Cordelia between them. The swings from violence to tenderness and back are the person whom Lear will die being:

> A plague upon you, murderers, traitors all!
> I might have saved her: now she's gone for ever!—
> Cordelia, Cordelia! Stay a little. Ha?
> What is't thou say'st?—Her voice was ever soft,
> Gentle and low, an excellent thing in woman.—
> I killed the slave that was a-hanging thee.   (5.3.281–6)

When he killed whoever hung Cordelia, Lear found the noble anger he prayed for earlier, but the gesture was empty, changing nothing. What lingers from his speech is his evocation of her voice: 'ever soft, / Gentle and low'. That is how we want to remember Cordelia; other questions about her no longer seem to matter.

A small mercy is that Lear recognizes Kent, who reveals that he has been with him all along in disguise as his servant Caius. Kent's description of what he has done—'That from your first of difference and decay / Have followed your sad steps' (5.3.302–3)— is a final repetition of the word Kent first used when he told the insolent Oswald 'I'll teach you differences' (1.4.84). Lear has lived through differences, and we who have read or watched the play have learned multiple differences: differences between the many forms of love, between the two faces of authority, between fidelity and trifling, between anger that has a claim to be noble and infantile anger that rages at whatever fails to fit its desires, between what language can express and what lies beyond words, between suffering that finds some purpose and suffering that feels victim to wanton gods; and neither last nor least, the differences that divide selves both within themselves and between each other.

Then come Lear's last words:

> And my poor fool is hanged! No, no, no life?
> Why should a dog, a horse, a rat have life,
> And thou no breath at all? Thou'lt come no more.
> Never, never, never, never, never!
> Pray you undo this button: thank you, sir.
> Do you see this? Look on her, look, her lips,
> Look there, look there!   (5.3.323–9)

On that, Lear dies. Once, wanting to join Poor Tom in unaccommodated wretchedness, he commanded others to help him; now he requests, meekly. Does Lear confuse his Fool, whom he says is hung, with Cordelia? His confusion showed when Kent asked him if he remembers Caius and he replied: 'He's dead and rotten' (5.3.299). Kent has to correct him. Lear's account being unreliable, each of us is left to decide where the Fool has gone. *Look there, look there!* leads some to believe Lear dies happy in the hope that Cordelia lives. As with the fate of the Fool, we understand Lear dying the death we can tolerate imagining. My sense of Lear's death depends on him knowing exactly what he says in his repetitions of *never*. The earlier Quarto version of the play has Lear speak three repetitions of *never*. The Folio increases that to five, making the repetition of *never* the centrepiece of the speech. *Never* is what echoes in our memory, as we put down our reading or leave the theatre; *never* is what Shakespeare asks us to live with, but *never* is not the last word.

Kent speaks what is both a plea and an epitaph. Whose heart Kent wills to break, Lear's, his own, or both, seems scarcely to matter.

KENT:	Break, heart, I prithee, break.
EDGAR:	Look up, my lord.
KENT:	Vex not his ghost: O, let him pass! He hates him
	That would upon the rack of this tough world
	Stretch him out longer.
EDGAR:	He is gone, indeed.
KENT:	The wonder is he hath endured so long:
	He but usurped his life. (5.3.331–8)

The play's final metaphor describes life as torture: being stretched upon a rack, which recalls Lear's earlier metaphor of being bound upon a wheel of fire. Kent then uses a verb, *usurp*, that poses another of the play's profound questions: Can a life reach a length that usurps—makes illegal use of—life? I will return to usurp. Kent always saw what was best in Lear: his will to life, his endurance, his authority as a source of order. Saying 'usurp', does Kent now perceive Lear as having lived too long, thereby precipitating the destruction of the younger lives he should have cared for?

Albany resigns his claim to rule 'the gored state' (5.3.342) in favour of Edgar and Kent. His words are a crucial reminder that we have seen more than a tragedy of individuals or families: an entire state has been gored. Tragedy, in its Greek origins, serves to effect the moral repair of a city or state that has been damaged, most often by war. Shakespeare expresses no specific political agenda, but throughout *King Lear* he calls us to reckon with authority, power, and equality of distribution. Individual vulnerability is always tied to collective vulnerability. As much as the family drama fills the play's foreground, we, in whatever time we live, have parts to play in the continual repairing of our own political state. In whatever form of violence we see our state gored, *King Lear* bears witness to that.

Kent in turn resigns his claim to rule, his words compounding the tragedy as they foretell another death that I find useless:

> I have a journey, sir, shortly to go:
> My master calls me. I must not say no.   (5.3.343–4)

Who then speaks the final speech? In the 1608 Quarto, Albany does. In the 1623 Folio the same words are spoken by Edgar, who now assumes leadership. We can make something of this change, or maybe not. Maybe, in the restoration of ceremony, the speakers are interchangeable; what matters is only that the words be spoken.

To me the words have a detached formality, the rhyming couplets sounding formulaic:

> The weight of this sad time we must obey:
> Speak what we feel, not what we ought to say.
> The oldest hath borne most: we that are young
> Shall never see so much nor live so long.   (5.3.345–8)

Yet I remember these words and quote them to myself. These last words explicitly privilege feeling, but the words have the formal tone of what ought to be said as the first gesture of repair. Their tone is that of someone who has been rendered numb by what he has just seen, yet who still must speak—the repair of the gored state begins by observing ceremony. Whether Edgar or Albany, the speaker's pain is too immediate to do what the words call for: to speak what he feels. The moment is one of those when we humans are not yet able to speak what is the worst. Saying what ought to be said and saying what is felt each has its claim, and we have to learn differences.

Lear's repetitions of *never* spoke what he felt, and seemed to render empty whatever anyone could say after. Yet these closing words are not empty; they leave us with final contradictions. Have the oldest really borne the most? Cordelia has given up most; has not Edgar seen more than any other? The unravelling began with Cordelia's attempt to say what she felt, not what she ought to say. Lear's response to Cordelia suppressed the love he felt, saying instead what his position compelled him to say. Every inch a king.

7

HOW *KING LEAR* HELPS

To best describe how I feel as I close the book or leave the theatre after *King Lear*, I turn to another of Shakespeare's plays. Here is part of the speech by Nick Bottom, the weaver and very amateur actor, when he rejoins his fellows after he was taken by the fairies, transformed into a creature with the head of an ass, and given to be the lover of Titania, their queen. From *A Midsummer Night's Dream*:

> I have had a most rare vision. I had a dream, past the wit of man to say what dream it was. Man is but an ass, if he go about to expound this dream... The eye of man hath not heard, the ear of man hath nor seen, man's hand is not able to taste, his tongue to conceive, nor his heart to report, what my dream was. I will... write a ballad of this dream: it shall be called 'Bottom's Dream', because it hath no bottom.   (*Midsummer Night's Dream*, 4.1.197–205)

Bottom's dream is comic to the point of absurdity; the dream that is *King Lear* is tragic to the point of grotesque. Yet finishing *King Lear*, I share Bottom's feeling that I have had a most rare vision, a dream that is past my wit to say what it was. And that, right there, might be the best response to the question of what *King Lear* offers to those who seek consolation. *Lear* offers us a dream, and when we want or need it, a chance to dream again. This dream is bottomless, because each time we dream it will reflect our need at that time.

As this book reaches the place where conclusions are expected, Bottom's speech is also a warning: how to conclude without expounding, if to *expound* is to propose some explanation or theory. Shakespeare does not write to solve, or resolve, or absolve. Shakespeare promises only drama—suspenseful anticipation of how actions undertaken in the face of threat will turn out. Drama lends itself to vulnerable reading because it enacts how one suffering person feels: distinct in her or his own circumstances, threatened, uncertain what awaits, able to make choices but having to act in response to fellow actors who share the stage.

Shakespeare casts an ironic smile at those who presume to solve. His consolations come from what I found years ago in my experience with the Chagall image of Jacob, described at the beginning of this book: the opportunity to walk into a story, inhabit it for a while, and then have that story, its language, and its characters continue to live with you.

*   *   *

There is also no bottom to human vulnerability: those who feel vulnerable are a multitude, diverse in what consoles them. Some find solace in Edgar's motivational aphorism that 'Men must endure / Their going hence, even as their coming hither' (5.2.10–11). The aphorism earns its authority by our seeing Edgar and Gloucester endure what they go through. But among the multitude of the vulnerable, others prefer to confront adversity. They feel affirmed by Cordelia's aggressive defiance to 'outfrown false fortune's frown' (5.3.7). Still others want what the Fool offers Lear: 'to out-jest / His heart-struck injuries' (3.1.9–10). Until we reach the moment of need, I believe none of us knows what will console us, and then our needs keep changing. We are each like Shakespeare's characters: impossible to draw a line around.

Shakespeare's writing can be therapeutic, even if he is nobody's therapist. He is a showman with this difference: his shows leave us feeling we have been more than entertained. Seeing the show doesn't solve anything, but it can instigate unpredictable changes, subtle beyond notice. The accumulation of those changes gives us what Nick Bottom has: more than the memory of a rare vision, it's the sense of still living on the edges of that vision.

* * *

Without pretending to expound what is bottomless, the rest of this chapter proposes four overlapping, interwoven sorts of consolation that *King Lear* offers, and the next chapter proposes a fifth. These forms of consolation are both serious and provisional. I seriously believe these are some of the ways that *King Lear* can help. But the consolations I propose are nothing more than prompts for readers to adapt; they invite adding what you find consoling, and what you add is more important for you than what I propose.

My first consolations are found in Shakespeare's *words* as they come off the page and live an independent existence. When we recollect his words in different circumstances, they detach from their original speaker and become anyone's own, finding new applicability.

Second are consolations of the *story*. By story I mean a tale that can be retold in different words yet remain recognizably the same, even absorbing changes in what happens. Just as Shakespeare's words work out of context, his stories are continually retold as happening in different times and places—he himself is retelling most of his stories from earlier versions. Vulnerable reading is transported by the story, but it also transports the story to the place of its present need.

Third are what I call consolations of *elsewhere*. *King Lear* takes us into its own half Elizabethan and half out-of-time elsewhere. We can move around in that space and vicariously experience shifts of identity. Lingering for a while in Shakespearean elsewhere can enable us to return to our own world with changed perceptions of what life confronts us with, and an enlarged sense of how we might respond.

Fourth are consolations of *transcendence*. The gods are continually invoked in *Lear*; what are these gods and in what ways do they care for us? Or do they merely toy with us, as Gloucester at his lowest point believes? What does *Lear* suggest about human suffering in relation to whatever lies beyond the visible, palpable materiality of world and flesh?

Finally, discussed in the chapter after this, are consolations of *King Lear*'s characters as they become people we come to care for, and—strange as it sounds—how we can come to feel some of these characters care for us.

The Solace of the Words

Early in the Covid-19 pandemic, when vulnerability meant not knowing how bottomless the disaster might become, the Folger Shakespeare Library produced a podcast in their *Shakespeare Unlimited* series with the title 'Shakespeare and Solace'. I was surprised that the discussion focused solely on particular lines, quoted without context, and not on stories or characters. Professional Shakespeareans found the first solace of Shakespeare to be in his words.

The episode's moderator, Barbara Bogaev, opens with a question that underlies what I call vulnerable reading: 'Because I don't think it's a foregone conclusion that you would turn to Shakespeare for solace necessarily,' she says, 'do you ... find yourself turning to Shakespeare in times of crisis, and if you do, what are you looking for?' Michael Witmore, the Folger's Director, elaborates, repeating what's not obvious about turning to Shakespeare for solace: 'I think Shakespeare has actually got a pretty grim view of what human beings are capable of.' He continues that Shakespeare also offers a 'hopefulness' but doesn't pursue the question of how Shakespeare can convey hopefulness while presenting such a grim view of humans.

One response to this apparent contradiction is that the 'grim view' is what makes the hopefulness *true*, in Cordelia's sense of being true. The grim and the hopeful are not opposites; they depend upon each other: true hope arises only with the clearest recognition of all that is grim.

'I tend to think of short phrases,' Witmore continues, setting the agenda for what follows. 'They sometimes jump out at me, and they're not really ... what I want to hear from them or not the same as what they mean in the passage.' Witmore surprised me here. As thoroughly as he knows Shakespeare's works, he doesn't consciously try to recall a line. Instead, lines *jump out* at him, seemingly unchosen. To me, his metaphor suggests the lines are waiting somewhere, ready to show up when needed—I embrace that way of imagining words. Witmore then observes that the lines are often not what he wants to hear; or, I would say, not what he thought he wanted to hear until the line jumped out. When lines jump out, they redirect his sense of need.

Witmore also gives us permission to hear the line out of context: as lines jump out, they are 'not the same as what they mean in the passage'. The words take on a life of their own, no longer limited to what they meant when spoken by a particular character in a particular play. The line that jumps out disrupts consciousness, and disrupting troubled thoughts is one way the words console, enabling us to know these troubles differently. The rest of the podcast presents actors, directors, and scholars reading lines that bring them comfort. They add little commentary, allowing Shakespeare's words to speak differently to each of us.

A later podcast refers back to this episode on solace and points out that both the premise of the initial question—that people turn to Shakespeare in times of trouble—and Witmore's willingness to let lines speak out of context are Victorian in spirit. Nineteenth-century guides to living collected lines from Shakespeare's plays and arranged them by topic, with biblical quotations on the facing page. That was a new elevation of Shakespeare's authority and a new way of using his writing. Losing the Victorians' need to align Shakespeare with the Bible, I'm happy to understand this book and the idea of vulnerable reading as reviving this older way of using Shakespeare.

* * *

King Lear has multiple lines that we might expect would occur to us when we need consolation, but recall Witmore's reflection that what will jump out is not necessarily what we expect: neither Shakespeare nor human consciousness works according to our expectations. We might expect, for example, that Lear's metaphor, 'I am bound / Upon a wheel of fire, that mine own tears / Do scald like molten lead' (4.6.46–8), would express our own suffering. Or that Kent's recognition of the sheer weight of suffering, 'man's nature cannot carry / Th'affliction nor the fear' (3.2.48–9), would offer sympathetic acknowledgement. Or that Lear's pleading question, 'Who is it that can tell me who I am?' (1.4.203), would remind us that another soul once felt so lost. Or that Cordelia's 'We are not the first / Who with best meaning have incurred the worst' (5.3.4–5) would lessen the feeling of being singled out in ill fortune. Perhaps these lines will jump out at us—but possibly others will.

Other lines give us words that enable us to speak what is worst. Gloucester's most sceptical outburst, 'As flies to wanton boys are we to th'gods: / They kill us for their sport' (4.1.41–2), is a metaphor of despair that offers us permission to call out what oppresses us, even the gods themselves. When all seems to be out of anyone's control, Gloucester's ''Tis the times plague, when madmen lead the blind' (4.1.54) reminds us it was ever so and finds an ironic humour that depicts oppression as absurdity. At what feels like an end, when there seems we have nowhere to be led, we can turn to Lear's response when Gloucester asks to kiss his hand: 'Let me wipe it first: it smells of mortality' (4.5.143).

Gloucester's and Lear's words give us something we can say when our own words are not enough; they give us second voices when our own speech fails us. When I speak Shakespeare's words in my situation, the words are both mine and not mine, in uncanny relation. The words express me better than I can express myself, but borrowed words set my self-expression aslant, giving me distance from my situation while I remain fully engaged in it.

The bitterness of many of Shakespeare's words enables us to give voice to our own bitterness when the expression of it is denied. Too often, those on whom the vulnerable depend—family members and professionals alike—assert their own version of Edgar's 'What, in ill thoughts again?' (5.2.10). Their caring comes with a demand for emotional compliance. Quoting Shakespeare is a strategy for telling the truth of ill thoughts, but at a remove. Like the Fool's riddles and jokes, quotations make truth at least unobjectionable and possibly tolerable.

Perhaps most important, the elevation of Shakespeare's language dignifies our feelings, giving them due intensity. His words remind us what humans are capable of, in speech, thought, and feeling. Shakespeare *ennobles* suffering, but without sentimentalizing or romanticizing it.

Shakespeare's own answer to the question of how words console might be Edgar's 'the worst is not / So long as we can say "This is the worst"' (4.1.31–2). So long as we can still *say*, so long as we can recall and speak the line, that makes the moment not yet the worst. Edgar realizes that the very worst is when we can no longer speak; when suffering and pain become all consuming, beyond representation. Dramatic tragedy happens at the limits of representation. It pushes those limits as it shows people in the most horrific situations—Gloucester just after his eyes are gouged out—still able to speak of what is worst. Speaking does not make the worst go away; that's not the point. As I struggle to say what such speaking of the worst does do, how it enables persevering, I fall back on a word like *dignity*, a word better exemplified than defined.

What I mean by dignity is Gloucester, after what has been done to him, still being able to compose the metaphor that compares the gods to wanton boys who torment, or Lear still able to express his pain through his metaphor of the wheel of fire. By making what oppresses them the subject of their chosen words, Gloucester and Lear make themselves more than its victims; that is their dignity. Here, dignity is no abstract principle but a performance; we know it as we hear Gloucester enact it. And then we can make his lines our own, saying them on our own behalf.

*   *   *

I cannot know what words might jump out at me, some day when I need comfort, but I hope to remember the lines near the end of Lear's poetic fantasy of how he and Cordelia might live together in prison. 'We two alone will sing like birds i'th'cage' (5.3.10), he says:

> And take upon's the mystery of things,
> As if we were God's spies.   (5.3.17–18)

Those are the lines I want coming to me in the time and place where I am at my most vulnerable. I choose them because I don't yet know what they mean; they leave me something to discover, then.

The words speak of 'the mystery of things', and the phrase 'God's spies' is itself a mystery. Lear is denying reality, but in his delusion I hear the peculiar sanity of a Zen koan. The teacher asks: *How do we take upon us the mystery of things?* The student is expected to respond, but response is impossible because whatever is said about mystery risks reducing what mystery is. The koan is a form of question that requires expounding what cannot be expounded, to use Nick Bottom's word again; koans set up students to make an ass of themselves, until they learn how not to. The seriousness of the Zen student's dilemma recalls Cordelia's struggle to speak love without betraying it. One way of responding while still affirming the mystery would be to answer: *By becoming God's spies.*

The Consolations of Story

Shakespeare's words, exactly those words, matter—until they don't, which happens sooner than we might think. Just as Shakespeare's words can live outside their story, his stories lend themselves to being retold in different words and in different worlds. Shakespeare is adapted not only in more or less free translations of his plays but also in media that include prose retellings, operas, fictional reimaginings, films, and graphic novels. His characters are adapted to give voice to vulnerabilities and violences of gender, disability, race, and colonial power that Shakespeare recognizes but treats ambivalently. Adaptations omit his words in part or entirely, and they change the plot, much as he changed the earlier anonymous *King Leir*. Some of my favourite 'Shakespeare' are adaptations in which the story remains, recirculating in a new but familiar form. For the person whom the story consoles, it ceases to matter in what sense the adaptation is authentic to a text or authorship.

Some quality of old narratives—to name it we might recycle the word *archetypal*—draws us to retell them when our lives have lost their sense of place—the sense of where we are in which story. Biblical stories, fables and folktales, and Shakespeare have this archetypal quality most consistently but not uniquely. We can set these archetypal narratives in different places, repopulate them with characters analogous to the originals but also distinctive to the new setting, shift the action to fit the times, and the old narrative becomes a new story that works in us and for us.

I see my family story reflected in *King Lear*, and I see the politics of my time reflected there as well. Or, better than the metaphor of reflection, the old narrative *bears witness* to present troubles. *Lear* bears witness specifically to what humans have gone through since we organized ourselves into families and states in which ownership orders relations between persons. Ownership creates the power to dispense, and dispensing becomes confused with giving. Property in whatever form—the size of each's share and their ability to control that share—instigates rivalry within generations and tensions between them.

King Lear is a story all about property—Lear divides his lands and loses his knights, Cordelia and Edgar lose their lands—until it isn't. It begins with how much opulence goes to whom, but that shades into other issues: how identities and authority are sustained by props that are purchased; how distribution meets or fails to meet human need; who is *true* to another person; and the list goes on. Yet at its end, the story is about the inevitable moment when property no longer matters. When Lear makes his final entrance, holding Cordelia, he has forgotten shares and their opulence. When the battle is fought, forgiveness exchanged, and final griefs incurred, property no longer matters. After the battle, whatever form that battle takes, it's about who holds whose body in their arms and how the living recall the voices of the dead. *Lear* helps me to remember that, too.

The Consolations of Elsewhere

Simply being able to go somewhere else for the duration of a performance, whether read or attended, is significant consolation.

A good story constructs its own world, and we who hear the story feel transported to that world. We take up provisional residence there: characters become people we know, and we begin to understand how that world makes such people possible. We then imagine what kind of person we might be, living in that world. Storms that wash you up on a strange shore force you to become someone else, according to what these different shores require. Our imagination of being in that different world is what I call *elsewhere*.

Another difference to learn is between escapes and escapism: does the time we spend in the imagined elsewhere affect us on our return and continue to affect us? The characters in *King Lear* show us ways we might learn to live, while transported elsewhere. All the characters are always on the move, relentlessly pursued or pursuing. Edgar is forced to the furthest elsewhere, and he is my model of how to return as more than one was.

Edgar has to move fast into a different world of hollow tree trunks and hovels, feeling lucky to find them. He lets go of enough of the old Edgar to enable himself to survive, but he holds onto enough so that when fortune offers an opening, he can restore himself. *Elsewhere*, as Edgar finds it, begins in necessity and opens into possibility; it demands real loss, but it extends real promises. Converting himself into Poor Tom, living in that world, he remakes himself as Edgar. His song of the road at the beginning of Act IV—'Yet better thus, and known to be contemned, / Than still contemned and flattered' (4.1.1–2)—immediately proves naive in its exuberance, but there's validity in its claim to change.

Edgar exemplifies the theologian Rowan Williams's argument that *catharsis*, Aristotle's distinguishing feature of tragedy that everyone understands a bit differently, 'demands the loss of the self'.[1] Williams writes that characters in tragedy 'are involved in understanding that growth, movement in time, entails a letting go of past identities'. If I understand Williams—or as I want to understand him—the audience's or reader's sense of catharsis begins in the characters' catharsis. *Elsewhere* is where this letting go of the self is demanded, but also where it is made possible.

As we, readers or audience, go to Shakespeare's elsewheres, we learn discernment in choosing whose mobility of self we invest in: here are more differences for the play to teach us. Letting go of past identities is not, in itself, a model necessarily worth following. Edmund lets go of his past identity with a literal vengeance, manipulating people and circumstances to fit his imagined elsewhere. By contrast, Edgar gives himself up to the elsewhere he is forced into, serving those he finds there. But I fear I am on the verge of making Edgar the character I want him to be—the triumphant survivor.

The elsewhere of *King Lear* is not a place of heroes; it is how Lear describes it:

> When we are born, we cry that we are come
> To this great stage of fools. (4.5.188–9)

Going to a performance of *King Lear* offers more than respite, more than time out, from the stage of fools that we call *real life*—a phrase I believe Shakespeare would consider to be one of our most foolish, because the line it seeks to draw as solid is actually porous. Shakespeare consoles by showing us that porousness and teaching us how to work with it.

King Lear is not a self-help book, and vulnerable reading should resist a tendency to push it in that direction. Shakespeare promises nothing more than a show about characters living elsewhere; he never claims he will change your life. But if my life or yours is to change, that might begin with a sense that we can go elsewhere and identify with characters who, thrown into situations they never expected, are able to let go of past identities. Then, in the elsewheres that our lives throw us into, necessity might be the beginning of creativity.

Consolations of Transcendence

By transcendence I refer to the timelessly recurring human imagination that, to paraphrase Hamlet after he's seen the Ghost, there is more to heaven and earth than all our rational senses can fathom or our words express. As humanity confronts a bottomless universe, we feel compelled to imagine various gods whose first act was to shape the dark shapelessness. Among all of Shakespeare's plays, *King Lear* asks most insistently: Where are the gods in all this? *What is the gods' cause?*

I will not catalogue all the instances where the gods are called upon in *Lear*. Sometimes the gods are invoked to lend force to what is said, but Shakespeare then questions what is invoked. When Kent protests Lear's banishment of Cordelia, Lear doubles down: 'Now, by Apollo—'. Kent interrupts: 'Thou swear'st thy gods in vain' (1.1.164, 166). How broadly do we take Kent's meaning? Is it only in this instance that swearing by the gods is in vain, because here and now Lear misrecognizes differences between his daughters' love or lack of it, or is Kent saying more than he himself is able to recognize? Is swearing by the gods, or petitioning them, *always* in vain, because that is not what gods are for, if the gods are there at all?

A different appeal to transcendence is made, and immediately undercut, when characters seek explanations in cosmic events. Gloucester, while struggling to make sense of Lear banishing Cordelia and Kent and nearly convinced by Edmund that Edgar is plotting against him, looks to the heavens. 'These late eclipses in the sun and moon portend no good to us' (1.2.94–5), he begins, going on for another ten lines. He exits, and Edmund speaks an aside in which I imagine I hear Shakespeare's voice:

> This is the excellent foppery of the world, that when we are sick in fortune—often the surfeits of our own behaviour—we make guilty of our disasters the sun, the moon and stars, as if we were villains on necessity, fools by heavenly compulsion … My father compounded with my mother under the dragon's tail and my nativity was under Ursa Major, so that it follows I am rough and lecherous. I should have been that I am had the maidenliest star in the firmament twinkled on my bastardizing. (1.2.108–21)

Edmund's words recall Cassius's much quoted lines in *Julius Caesar*: 'Men at some time are masters of their fates. / The fault, dear Brutus, is not in our stars / But in ourselves' (1.2.145–7). By blaming the eclipses Gloucester displaces responsibility away from himself and his fellow courtiers who passively watch things unravel. The fault is in themselves.

Edmund might call Gloucester's 'As flies to wanton boys are we to th'gods' (4.1.41) more foppery: unable to give up the gods, Gloucester now finds them malign. Actually, Cornwall and Regan tortured Gloucester for *their* sport. And sport it was, because they gained no information or tactical advantage from what they did. But here, Gloucester's words are not foppery: the injuries he feels—both blindness and betrayal—must be cried out, and he must believe his cry is heard; humans must believe something hears them.

Beyond the contradictions and uncertainties in how the gods are invoked, *King Lear*'s understanding of transcendence may be most revealed when the gods are *not* called upon, notably in the play's ending. When Kent foretells his own imminent death, it is Lear, 'My master', who calls him, not the gods or any divine necessity. When Lear, holding Cordelia's dead body, questions justice—'Why should a dog, a horse, a rat have life, / And thou no breath at all?' (5.3.324–5), he does not address this question to the gods. The question simply hangs there, unanswerable, witnessed only by those standing by, each alone as he confronts the horror. 'Never, never, never, never, never!' is all Lear can say, before his final delusion that Cordelia might still live. This closing scene shows pure absence, not even malicious gods are present. In an age when the imperative of faith was unquestioned—however bitter the contests over which faith—the scandal of *King Lear* is to render the gods first as empty words and then, worse yet, as irrelevant.

It's curious to me, reading *King Lear* in my own time, how much ink was once spilled over whether and how it might be a distinctly Christian drama. That says most about the commitments of the critics and their times, yet Shakespeare invites the question. In Cordelia's reentry scene in Act IV, we cannot ignore the biblical resonance of her line 'O dear father, / It is thy business that I go about' (4.3.25–6, referencing Luke 2:49). Cordelia's line is not, however, one in which I hear Shakespeare speaking through his character. Cordelia uses biblical language to express her own imagination of who she is in relation to the father she now imagines Lear to be. Biblical words enable her to speak the part that she casts herself to play; she makes them her own.

Some of *King Lear*'s most thoughtful modern critics see no transcendence—only unrelenting bleakness—in *King Lear*'s existential vision. Jan Kott expresses this view:

> there is in *King Lear* only "Macbeth's stage". On it, people murder, butcher and torture one another, commit adultery and fornication, divide kingdoms. From the point of view of a Job who has ceased to talk to God, they are clowns. Clowns who do not yet know they are clowns.[2]

Kott's understanding of *Lear* is compelling but seems incomplete. Rowan Williams confronts the emptiness at the end of *Lear* in terms that at first seem complementary to Kott's: 'we seek an explanation of appalling suffering, but it is precisely the lack of explanation that makes it genuinely appalling'.[3] Nor would an explanation help: 'It is the *kind* of problem it is precisely because explanation could not make it better,' Williams writes. If not explanation, and if the urge to make it better is often a form of denial, then what? How do we respond to what we read or see as Lear holds his senselessly murdered daughter? To this question, Williams offers me more than Kott.

At the end of *King Lear*, Edgar survives, and unlike Kent he will go on surviving. I think primarily of Edgar when I read how Williams describes a form of tragic survival:

> there may be a future in which the unaltered memory of hurt comes to be lived with in unpredictable ways, without wholly destructive consequences. But to arrive at such a moment…you have first to give up any hope of explanation or compensation.[4]

Williams makes the same point when he describes what he calls the 'thinking self' as 'what it is that holds the memory of loss and trauma without collapsing'.[5] For me, this self that holds its memories without collapsing is better called the well-weathered self, or the self after the storm, or—free of metaphor—the surviving self: the self that crafts, and continues crafting, its own survival. This self is not one of Kott's clowns, however grotesque its story may be.

Lear cannot hold so much loss and trauma without collapsing. His affliction in Cordelia's death is too much, and his heart breaks. Kent might become a surviving self, but he cannot imagine the possibility of what Williams looks for: living with the memory of hurt 'without wholly destructive consequences'. Memory of the deaths he has been unable to prevent overwhelms him. Thus his death strikes me as sadder than Cordelia's, at least after I close the book and reflect on what has happened. For her, death validates her cause as right; Kent's death feels like acquiescence to the failure of Lear's cause.

At a certain age—which for me means being just short of Lear's age—self-reflection requires living with memories of hurt: in part what others did to us, in another part where we simply got a bad roll of the dice that Shakespeare calls fortune, but most painful of all, what we have done to ourselves and others. *King Lear* is a fable describing different ways to accumulate such memories of hurt, and at the end is the question of how to live with these memories. To whom do we cry out our hurts, and from what do we expect a response? Characters in *Lear* use religious language as a resource to express what they must make sense of, whether that is Gloucester calling the gods malign or Cordelia claiming to be about her father's business. To respect the real work that religious language does for these characters does not require believing in a transcendental domain lying behind this language. Human imaginations, responding to shared need, collaborated to create that language. Shakespeare is one of those imaginations.

King Lear is all I need of the transcendental, yet I need the theologian, Williams, to give me words to say how *Lear* is enough. Williams is truest to Shakespeare when he offers not an explanation but a nonrhetorical question, one that demands a lived response, not more words. Tragedy, of which *Lear* is exemplary, asks: After all the horror that has been shown, 'what endures of our humanity?'[6] In *Lear*, this question is embodied in the figure of Poor Tom. Listen again to how Tom is described. 'I'th'last night's storm I such a fellow saw, / Which made me think a man a worm' (4.1.37–8), says Gloucester. Lear addresses Tom as being 'the thing itself:…such a poor bare, forked animal' (3.4.100–2). Tom is what endures of humanity when the human is reduced to being thought a worm; Tom is the thing itself. And Edgar endures being Tom. Edgar is resilient, but any claim his resilience has on us as an exemplar remains embodied in Poor Tom, always cold and driven into a madness that I believe is beyond counterfeiting. At the end, Edgar gives no grand, charismatic speech. We cannot be sure how damaged he remains.

Williams insists, as it would be false to *King Lear* not to insist, that the tragic imagination is *not* a 'celebration of the noble and indomitable human spirit'. What consoles is far more modest: 'we have not been silenced forever by loss'.[7] That is why I believe Edgar, who has most right to feel silenced, ought to speak the play's last words, and why these words should not be some lyrical, inspiring speech. Elevated words risk seeking either to explain or to make it better. They risk making the moment their occasion, making it about themselves. What matters is that Edgar speak at all: that he is not silenced by the images of horror he has seen or by what has been inflicted on his body. His speaking is sufficient in itself, just as *King Lear* is sufficient in itself. Any word like *transcendence* is unsatisfactory; what it points toward is beyond language. By the ending of *Lear* I no longer need such a word.

What I need is the consolation of seeing Edgar reemerge out of Poor Tom and take upon himself what will, for him, be the burden of authority, not its entitlement. 'O, see, see' (5.3.322) says Albany, directing us to Lear, whose speech then ends with 'Look there, look there!' (5.3.329). What should we see? Shakespeare calls us to witness what endures of our humanity: what can still speak and hope. At the end we close the book or leave the theatre having seen ourselves naked but not collapsing. We see ourselves enduring to live in unpredictable ways.

8

TRAGIC SHARING

Among *King Lear*'s many consolations, I care the most for how its characters become my companions. Just as Shakespeare's words come to us no longer limited by their original context, and just as his stories invite adaptation, so too may his characters step out of the play they contingently inhabit. Companions sometimes comfort us, sometimes guide us, sometimes allow us to see ourselves reflected in our differences from them—and sometimes they just amuse us. Imagining *Lear*'s characters as my companions risks making them be who I want them to be, yet they truly can speak in their own voices. They can talk back to us, if we learn to listen.

Lear's characters remain strange to me: violently impelled in their extremes of loyalty and betrayal, uncompromising. But each also mirrors some disposition of mine, allowing me to acknowledge it. Companionship lives in this balance: what the character mirrors enables closeness to the character, but their alien strangeness saves me from the narcissism of seeing only myself. The alien aspect can be uncomfortable; the mirroring aspect can get too comfortable. A good companion is comfortable enough of the time, but sufficiently uncomfortable to keep our relationship provocative. Odd as it sounds to say about literary characters, I feel their interest to me depends on how interesting

I can be to them. When I show characters that I recognize who they are—what they struggle with, what long-engrafted condition limits them in their struggles, what they value and desire, where they succeed and what makes their failures seem inevitable—I enable them to show me more of myself.

To begin the dialogue that is companionship, I write this chapter as letters that address each character directly as *you*. Letters hope for a response; they do not claim the last word. Just as Michael Witmore said he was surprised at which of Shakespeare's lines jump out at him when he needs solace, so I expect to be surprised who answers me some day, saying what I least expect.

These letters are a way of working toward Rowan Williams's suggestion: *'there may be a future in which the unaltered memory of hurt comes to be lived in unpredictable ways'*. The longer I consider that, the more I believe Williams expresses where vulnerable reading leads. His statement is an article of faith, in the sense that I have to believe it is true in order to do what I must to make it come true. Unpredictable as our future is, we can give ourselves resources that may prove useful in encountering it; Shakespeare's words, his stories, and his characters are such resources. *Lear's* characters and I both have what Williams calls memories of our hurts: I come to share theirs as I retell their stories, and they eventually share mine. How that happens is the process known as tragedy.

For me tragedy as a literary genre is secondary to tragedy as a form of human relationship, extending to collective participation. Tragedy is better called *tragic sharing*: a dialogue of hurts, first among the characters—represented in the shock and pain that Albany, Kent, and Edgar feel jointly at the end of *Lear*—then between characters and readers or audience. Tragic sharing is modelled on theatrical participation but extends beyond the theatre. Much remains uncertain about how the ancient Greeks experienced their tragic theatre, but we know they took tragedy seriously as a ritual for acknowledging collective pain. Shakespeare's tragedies also recognize that need. Even solitary reading should retain a sense of participating in a communal experience. We read with awareness that others have said these words before, both aloud on stage and silently in private moments. Their experiences resonate in ours.

Tragic sharing refuses to look away from what we least want to see, and it refuses to separate the other's hurt from our own. Tragic sharing does not excuse human agency when people hurt each other, but it understands that individuals never fully control how they feel compelled to act. Tragic performance, on page or stage, enables us to look our vulnerability in the face, and if what we see frightens us—as it probably should—then tragic sharing is a way to accept that fear as what we ought to feel and what we are not alone in feeling. Tragedy teaches that viable hope can arise only by first accepting all that is hopeless, and a mature appreciation of tragedy depends on that paradoxical recognition. The sadness of tragedy is watching people who do not yet know their own hopelessness. As we observe them failing to see where their actions are leading, we recognize ourselves and our potential to misrecognize.

The letters that follow are overtures to tragic sharing. They begin by asking what is asked throughout *King Lear*: *Who's there?* Good companionship keeps this question open; it refuses to draw boundaries around who people are and who they might become. We're always living in some kind of storm, separated from each other and half blinded by the rain. We never quite know who's there.

Asking who's there leads into whether I have properly *appreciated* the character. I thank them for expanding my ability to see people's different sides: showing me the flaws in those who are the best, and what led those who are worst to being worst. I thank them for helping me accept contradictions within myself. I thank them for resisting being whom I want them to be, pushing me to ask who they are there to be.

But then I must ask, *how far does our companionship go?* Companionship enables me to appreciate our differences, until those cross a boundary—here are more differences to be learned. Limits express my values: a value marks where our companionship needs to end. Without limits, I would eventually either force my companion to be the person I want them to be, or I would cease to be the person I feel I am here to be.

Finally, some of these letters express apology. I need to tell some characters that I recognize how Shakespeare has treated them badly by putting them into the situations he has and making them act as he has. That leads into the question of how I have treated different characters, as my retelling selectively narrates their part in *King Lear*. On this latter issue, readers will have to add their thoughts to what I have written, because my blind spots are just that. A dialogue does not seek to assert final conclusions; instead it invites elaboration. These letters begin dialogues not only with Shakespeare's characters, but with you who read my reading of Shakespeare. As you respond to these letters—whether you respond to me or to the character—my reading becomes your reading.

'Words, words, words,' Hamlet replies when Polonius asks what he is reading (*Hamlet*, 2.2.197). Shakespeare writes words for actors and directors to use as they create characters on stage. He writes only words, leaving to others the task of embodying them. We readers of *King Lear* have to play all the parts ourselves and imagine the stage they act on. Eventually we can invite characters to step off that stage into our lives. To become able to hear them, we first must learn to speak to them.

To Kent

When Lear asks why you, disguised as Caius, wish to serve him, you reply that his face has in it what you call authority. Whatever once was best in Lear's authority is most visible to me as it is reflected in your loyalty. Loyalty to Lear has, I imagine, made your capacity for violence noble. But authority lies not in anyone's countenance, even if that one is the king. Authority is a relationship. You enable Lear to be the king he is, you enable Cordelia to play the part she chooses, and they reciprocally enable you to act nobly. You are never more noble than when Lear abuses his authority and exiles you.

Among all the characters you belong most to your own time. Your faults—your unrestrainable anger and quickness to fight—are reflections of Lear, and in *Lear*'s world these are not faults but who you have to be. *Lear*'s time is a version of Shakespeare's time. On the streets outside his Globe, those aggressive qualities remained necessary but required a level of restraint that would have offended your sense of acting nobly. Noblemen still carried swords but had to know when to draw them; anger was losing its privilege. As Shakespeare's audience observed how your nobility and your volatility depend on each other, they saw a world still present and holding power, but fading. Some watched with nostalgia for what was being lost and others felt relief. The mixture of those feelings forms the sensibility of modernity, and so you still move us. For all that is antique about you, we're not past you yet.

But in your will to follow Lear in death I see a lesson in loyalty gone too far. Lear was an old man ripe for death; how he dies may be a tragedy, but not his death itself. Your final act of willing your own death is the culmination of who you are committed to being—committed to defining yourself by service to those whose authority you recognize—but it is also the limit of my companionship with you. From the perspective of my world, your sense of honour has a detectable smell of self-destructiveness. I have often shared your will to attach yourself to the authority of men like Lear. You reassure me that was well done, but I learn from you that I also did well to let go of those relationships when I did.

As much as you command my respect, I hope not to see too much of myself in you. You and Cordelia are both moralists, absolutely certain in your sense of what is right, and compelled to make the world conform to that sense. Both of you thus prefer death to compromise, and you don't count the cost of others' deaths. Your master's call is stronger than your will to live and discover whom you might serve after he's gone. I appreciate you as a caution against the unquestioning certainty of cause that you so nobly embody.

To Gloucester

No one deserves what Shakespeare puts you through. But in a tragic world, it's not a question of what anyone deserves. Shakespeare also lets you live long enough to see feelingly and to know your true son's love.

For me as a vulnerable reader, three moments define you. First is when you misrecognize Edmund as your ally and believe Edgar to be your enemy. Edmund plays to your greatest insecurity: your self-doubts about the love and fidelity of the person closest to you, and beyond that, doubt about whether you merit the authority you claim. Where we have most to lose, we most readily succumb to believing the worst. In your calamitous misrecognition of who is true, your actions reflect Lear's. In my life, the Edmund figure has not been another person but part of myself. It took me the longest to acknowledge my identification with you in our predatory self-doubt.

The second moment is on the cliff at Dover, when your only solution to desperation is to jump. I count that not as weakness on your part, but as another misrecognition: you do not know your guide for who he is. That's not entirely your fault; Shakespeare is setting you up. The cliff scene is Edgar's moment for which you provide the occasion. By unwittingly enabling Edgar to save you, you act as a parent should: you make possible a necessary part of your child's journey. I can imagine an adaptation of the story in which you do recognize Edgar as your guide, but you sustain the charade for his sake.

The third moment is yours alone, when you are blinded. You have enacted your version of Kent's loyalty, and your body suffers for that. Yours is the greatest physical vulnerability in *King Lear*. When you realize what Cornwall and Regan are going to do to you, you accept having no choice—'I am tied to th' stake and I must stand the course' (3.7.61). In the aftermath of this violence you gradually reopen yourself to Edgar—and to how much more I cannot say, because you tell us so little about what it's like to see feelingly. Your story is almost over by then. We don't have enough time to learn what you see. Is such sight more than your life can sustain? Is your journey to the cliff as far as anyone can go?

Your companionship lies in how you survive the worst and are not silenced. But your generosity is to let Edgar often speak for you. Your question, 'Now, good sir, what are you?', enables his description of both himself and you, that gives vulnerable readers an image of how they might think of themselves:

> A most poor man, made tame to fortune's blows,
> Who, by the art of known and feeling sorrows,
> Am pregnant to good pity.   (4.5.233–5)

Edgar then expresses what companionship offers: 'Give me your hand: / I'll lead you to some biding' (4.5.235–6). *Biding*: a place to dwell, to rest; a kind of home after the loss of home, where vulnerability hopes to find refuge, with a companion to lead there. Your need enables Edgar, who enables you to believe there can be such a place of biding, and you enable that belief in others.

When you say—and on my imagined stage, you sit under a tree—that a man can rot even here, I hear you exhausted, certainly, but more than that, at peace with yourself; it's your version of 'Let be'. I hope some day I can sit under my tree and say the same. I believe you die happy enough, knowing Edgar has more than forgiven you.

To Goneril and Regan

The two of you and Cordelia are all three every inch a king's daughters, but you two are the dark side of majesty. One question hangs over my thoughts of you: Did you push Lear into becoming the person who can curse you with such ugly, unrelenting vehemence, or did Lear's curses—once more subtle than we see them finally becoming—make you capable of the viciousness you eventually perpetrate? Shakespeare seems to tilt toward you being the villains: Cordelia says she knows you, 'what you are' (1.1.284). But she is hardly unbiased.

Shakespeare makes it easier to conflate your identities than to perceive your differences, and I compound his ill treatment of you by not writing you each a letter of your own. That conflation is not the worst of how Shakespeare treats you. What Dame Harriet Walter writes about playing Ophelia in *Hamlet* speaks to you in *Lear*:

> Imagine being given practically nothing to say in your own or in Ophelia's defence. Knowing, moreover, that 'the noble' Hamlet's treatment of Gertrude is similar, you can see how one starts to wonder whose side Shakespeare is really on. In fact, I have turned down the part of Gertrude…because she seems to me to be even more muzzled than Ophelia, who at least breaks out into a form of self-expression in her madness.[1]

Ophelia and Gertrude are assailed by a younger man; you are compelled to endure an older, dominating man spitting far worse insults into your face. Harriet Walter helps me begin to hear the silences that have been imposed upon you, the rage that builds within those silences, and what it means to have to treat your husband as your 'lord'.

What Walter says about Ophelia raises a question for you, Goneril and Regan: How much of your cruelty and violence is your way—the only way you can imagine—of breaking into a form of self-expression? That excuse wears thin when we get to Regan's enthused sadism in the blinding of Gloucester and later to

Goneril's poisoning of Regan. To call these acts self-expression wildly overcorrects Shakespeare's ill treatment of you. But ill treatment often produces selves whose means of expression is destruction.

*   *   *

You had to wait a long time, but finally you found a storyteller to give you voices. The novelist Jane Smiley writes about how she began to imagine retelling *King Lear* in her 1991 novel, *A Thousand Acres*:

> I still felt that Goneril and Regan had a point of view that somehow the play...had slighted...So I set about correcting my friend William Shakespeare—something no sane adult would attempt...I gave the daughters a rationale for their apparently cruel behavior. I gave Goneril a voice and Regan a point of view....And by the time I was finished with *A Thousand Acres*, I felt that in some ways Shakespeare and I were closer than ever. I knew that, like me, he had reworked found material, and that he had discovered the material to be more intractable than he expected it to be...I also learned...that William Shakespeare and I were not soul mates, that I was a twentieth-century woman and he was a sixteenth-century man. He expected the world to be a crueler place than I did—warlike.[2]

The backstory that Smiley gives you in *A Thousand Acres* makes the Lear character, Larry, a perpetrator of incest. The older daughter represses her memories of this, mostly, for a while. The middle daughter claims she offered herself to their father in order to protect their younger sister. That sister, having grown up not knowing at what cost she was protected, cannot comprehend her older sisters' attitude toward their father and how they eventually treat him. It's a fully told backstory, giving you what Shakespeare denies you, your own points of view.

Novels fill in such details; plays leave characters open to multiple realizations in performances by different actors. For all that you, Goneril and Regan, gain in sympathy as Smiley tells your story, for me your backstory risks making who you are too readily understandable; it limits you. On Shakespeare's stage you are wild: icy control suddenly giving way to uncontrollable violence. That dangerousness is muted by the clearer motivations of your reincarnations. They just don't scare me as you do.

* * *

What I think both of you love in Edmund is his male freedom, extending to the freedom to plot and betray. I understand your lust for him as being less sexual than a desire to embrace an identity you imagine to be free from all that constrains you. At first, you may love Edmund less than you want to be Edmund, to wear his pants. Later, you each love him because the other does: you have been raised by a father who puts you in competition with each other. You both know Edmund will eventually betray you, but you can't admit that—so you displace your expectation of betrayal onto each other. The closer you get to what you want, the faster you bring on your own destruction.

You choose your acts of violence; you are responsible. But your choices are products of your own long-engrafted condition. You act as the persons you believe you must be, and that's your humanity.

* * *

At the end of *The Tempest*, Prospero says of Caliban what Lear is never able to say of you his daughters: 'this thing of darkness I | Acknowledge mine' (5.1.309–10). I want to offer you that acknowledgement, which is not the same as forgiveness. You have responsibility for allowing your rage to make you things of darkness, but others owe you acknowledgement of their part in building that rage.

You, Goneril and Regan, are cautionary companions. You show me whose acknowledgement I will never have, but you shock me into finding a better way to live with that.

To Lear's Fool

Everyone deserves a fool, not to be the song-and-dance man you play at being, but for telling the truth as you do. Among all the characters, I remain least sure who you are. Lear isn't sure either: he alternatively patronizes you, comforts you, depends on you, and even loves you, but to his great loss, he never pays you serious attention. Then Shakespeare seems to forget about you. Or does he?

For me, your disappearance after the hovel is your last, best riddle: *What is gone but still present?* My guess is that playing the Fool is already your second self, and you can't transform yourself further, when that self no longer plays a part in the story. You give everything to playing that part, forget your first self in it, and finally the performance wears you out. By the time you get to the hovel, little of you seems left to disappear.

But you burn brightly: you tell the truth more directly than Cordelia, and you are as faithful as Kent. Your relationship to Lear might be the closest he comes—until the reconciliation with Cordelia—to showing what deserves to be called affection.

And then you are gone, remembered in Lear's last words with the final irony that he may be confusing you with Cordelia. For me you are better remembered in the lingering melody of your song:

'Though the rain it raineth every day' (3.2.80). Your singing is the truest consolation.

You proceed from being a jester to become the enigma at the core of *King Lear*: whether with one foot in another reality when you are present, or remaining a presence in your absence, you remind me how much more there is than I am able to see. I doubt whether Lear realized you were one of God's spies, there in his court all along, but maybe being with you is what turned his mind to that phrase. Thinking of you keeps me watching, knowing you can reappear in multiple guises.

To Cornwall's Servant, Who Tries to Stop Him

You show me the courage I lack. In *Hamlet*, Polonius's often quoted precept, 'to thine own self be true' (*Hamlet*, 1.3.81), is ironic, coming from a courtier whose self is least of all his own and who measures truth in the currency of royal favour. When you, who remain nameless, attempt to stop Cornwall from gouging out Gloucester's remaining eye, you show what being true to oneself can require. In that moment you must either refuse to be part of the horror that Cornwall perpetrates or be complicit in it. That moment is ethical life in its most naked form.

'But better service have I never done you / Than now to bid you hold' (3.7.82–3) you say, and for that Cornwall calls you a dog. You know full well the price you will pay, whether or not you stop Cornwall. In Lear's world, there's no reward for those whose actions show their lords what being true to yourself calls for.

As a companion, you are the substance of which words like integrity, conscience, and virtue are mere shadows.

To Cornwall

Some acts reduce their perpetrators to being someone who did *that* and that alone. Shakespeare chooses not to tell me anything about you that might mitigate how I judge your blinding of Gloucester—I see him wanting that act to stand unmitigated in its evil, its cruelty. Shakespeare reduces you to being a representation of the human capacity for atrocity. Companionship with you is thus more than limited: you are the limit at which there can be no companionship. You are less a person than a warning, like signs designating areas of toxic contamination: *Contact with what lies here will cause sickness and death.* Something must have driven you to such viciousness, or not. By Shakespeare telling us nothing about you, he may be expressing his darkest suspicion: some aspects of some selves are always there, inescapable, waiting for a moment to be unleashed. You and your servant are the human tension between violence and conscience.

Your death consoles me because it shows that in the end anger has no privilege, contrary to Kent's lame excuse for his aggressions. You and your servant—he who might have pulled you back—both find a fast route to an early grave, but it's you who deserves to be thrown on the dunghill. And, given how Regan's affections are tending, maybe you were.

To Albany

Conciliation is your signature gesture. Like me, maybe like Shakespeare, you readily let yourself be a spectator to your own life. Cornwall has no capacity for self-reflection, but you can get lost in endless reflections. I know you maybe too quickly.

For a long while, you let Goneril's deprecations define you. After Lear rides off with his knights, she insults you, presumably for the respect you have just shown Lear:

> No, no, my lord,
> This milky gentleness and course of yours
> Though I condemn not, yet, under pardon,
> You are much more at task for want of wisdom
> Than praised for harmful mildness.   (1.4.316–20)

It's a tangled, passive aggressive, doubly if not triply barbed insult, beginning by attributing feminine qualities—'milky gentleness'— to you. Then after a perfunctory disclaimer—'under pardon'— Goneril attacks, finding fault in your lack of wisdom and harm in your mildness. On all counts, she holds you a failure.

You acknowledge she may be right: 'How far your eyes may pierce I cannot tell: / Striving to better, oft we mar what's well' (1.4.321–2). But are those words as conciliatory as they seem? The first line can be heard as referring to the future that no one knows, and you acknowledge that Goneril may have a better sense of what will happen than you have. But you also might imply that Goneril has been plotting all along to take what Lear still holds. Your second line supports that, cautioning Goneril that her attempts to gain risk leaving her with less. She protests 'Nay, then—', you cut her off with more conciliation: 'Well, well, th'event' (1.4.323–4), meaning future events will show who's right. The dialogue preserves a veneer of civility, but barely. By Act IV the gloves have come off. But as soon as you answer Goneril insult for insult, you then take her side against Cordelia.

Goneril is not entirely wrong about you. When the final battle requires making a choice, you can be accused of fecklessness, even betrayal. You may have smiled when you heard Cordelia's army had landed (4.2.4–5), yet you still join forces with her sisters. Critics propose the excuse that for you, the foreignness of the French forces counted as an invasion, and the need to resist that overrode the justice of Cordelia's cause. I find that account of your motives plausible but not compelling. Joining Cordelia would have been no easy thing. But on my reading, you knew it was right and you didn't do it.

When you speak of your 'great love' for Goneril (1.4.287), I think you mean it, but as an expression of duty. Love is what you ought to feel; it's what your position demands and what you expect of yourself. Even when you know what Goneril is capable of, you cannot fight against her. I see you as perpetually caught in the middle: between duty to your wife despite her insults and the wrongness of her cause, and your duty to the right cause of Lear and Cordelia. In that middle there's scarcely space to breathe.

At the end you know that having taken the side you did, you bear some responsibility for the deaths of Cordelia and Lear. Maybe that's part of your final resignation—'Friends of my soul, you twain / Rule in this realm' (5.3.341–2). Resignation may be your most self-expressive gesture. I can imagine you living out your days in a monastery.

Goneril's gendered insults, casting you as feminine, show you caught between the old warrior masculinity and something too newly emerging to yet be recognizable as a different way of being a man; that is why you remain a character we need, as we live with that same problem. You let Edmund command your forces in the battle, then you let Edgar kill Edmund for you, although your cause is as great as his. Ultimately, you leave the field; again, resignation defines you, the only way you can imagine expressing what your conscience demands. You are the one character whom I can imagine talking to as a friend.

To Edmund

When Lear describes the human condition as 'this great stage of fools' (4.5.189), I see you laughing with appreciation that someone finally gets it right. You are the only character for whom laughter is your characteristic expression. But it doesn't save you from being driven by your resentments.

Many of Shakespeare's villains suffer from their innate talent running up against the limitations imposed by rigid hierarchy, but in this predicament you stand out. As Goneril and Regan are frustrated by being women, your frustration is being born a bastard. You will do anything to prove society's deprecation wrong. Edgar shifts his shape, but you are the greater trickster: too smart for your own good, you bring about your end. 'Or with a little shuffling' (*Hamlet*, 4.6.118), says Claudius as he plots how to get the poisoned blade into the hands of Laertes, whom he will use to kill Hamlet. Hamlet will stab Claudius with that blade. You too believe that a little shuffling can solve most of life's problems. That's the part of you I fear in myself.

You don't hate Edgar, who will treat you well when his time comes to be Earl. You hate the prospect of spending your life being subservient because of inheritance rules that are indifferent to actual ability. You don't love either Goneril or Regan; you love making them both love you. Maybe more, you love what is perilous about that situation. The game is seeing how you can get out of the dangers you create for yourself. The duel with the unknown champion is one danger too many. You give up playing the trickster because your need to prove yourself is bottomless. When you play the knight and accept the challenge as your final claim to the legitimacy of nobility, I think you know that contest does not favour your talents. But by then your plotting is played out, and at least fighting isn't boring.

Your parting line: 'Yet Edmund was beloved' (5.3.245)—is that sad or merely pathetic? Your idea of being beloved is: 'The one the other poisoned for my sake / And after slew herself' (5.3.246–7). You measure your self worth by the weight of others' destruction. Yet you try to do a last good deed, stopping the execution of Cordelia that you ordered. The messenger is too late. It's your evil that remains, its effects echoing in Lear's repetitions of 'Never'.

In letting you entertain me for so long, I recognize my own complicity.

To Edgar

I read *King Lear* as two stories: the bitter end of an old king and the dispensation that king represents, and the education of a young king who can initiate a new order. When Poor Tom meets Lear at the hovel on the heath, the two stories briefly merge, but it's an ironic merging because Lear does not know who Poor Tom really is. And at that point you, Edgar, hardly know who you are. When you and Lear meet again, he pays no attention to you. Yet you are his successor.

Lear's dispensation is founded on male absolutism backed by violence: to be noble is to fight and punish. When Lear's madness allows him a moment of political lucidity, he repudiates what he has been: 'Thou hast seen a farmer's dog bark at a beggar... And the creature run from the cur?' He then calls that 'the great image of authority: a dog's obeyed in office' (4.5.162–6). Your education as future king is to have been that beggar. You have been forced to run, barefoot, from the cur. At the end of *King Lear*, your story begins. The Folio version of the play is right to assign the last lines to you. Your future authority is expressed in the *Tao Te Ching*: 'whoever assumes a nation's misfortune is called the emperor of all beneath heaven'.[3] Poor Tom is your nation's misfortune. He remains a figure of every nation's misfortune.

In becoming Poor Tom you choose life. I hold you so important because among all the characters in *Lear* who are forced to live as someone different from the person they have been—Kent, Gloucester, Cordelia, and Lear himself—you embrace what is forced upon you, your second self, pronouncing 'Edgar I nothing am' (2.2.187). When my own vulnerabilities become realities, will I have the will to give up that much of myself? I once came close, but now I am older.

In the succession of selves that you assume—first Poor Tom, then Gloucester's two or maybe three guides, and finally the anonymous challenger to Edmund—you become Edgar reborn. During your service to your father as you 'Led him, begged for him, saved him from despair' (5.3.206), I see you discovering who you can be: You become someone able to lead without being Lear's great image of authority, a dog in office.

If, and that *if* is significant, in the ending of *King Lear* there is more than 'Never', I find it in the possibility expressed in Edmund's response to your tale of how you have escaped, survived, and served your father: 'This speech of yours hath moved me, / And shall perchance do good' (5.3.215–16). You who have seen the worst may be prepared to use authority for something better.

To Cordelia

You are the patron saint, perfected in your martyrdom, of people who have had enough and finally call out others for who they really are. When Lear offers you 'A third more opulent than your sisters" (1.1.85) in exchange for a performance of love, you reject his demand as confusing feeling with its expression and equating affection with property. Then you tell your sisters: 'I know you what you are' (1.1.284). For these truths and more, commentators on *King Lear* praise you: the question is not whether to sanctify you but how much. Maybe I resent the imperative to value your truth telling as all that matters about you; that draws too sharp a line around you.

I want to ask you, as a question, what Albany says to Goneril: 'How far your eyes may pierce I cannot tell' (1.5.321). Addressed to you, that becomes a dark question. How far can you foresee what human wreckage your actions will lead to—first, when you refuse to play Lear's love-test game, and later, when you lead the invasion? I fear you can see far indeed, and the losses cause you no second thought. I suspect you can see even to the likelihood of your death. If so, you play your part like a character in Greek tragedy: utterly uncompromising as you precipitate everyone's destruction.

If you are a saint, then for me that means being a holy terror. Your cause, first to defy Lear and then to restore him, counts no costs. For you, conviction is everything.

We know from Shakespeare's history plays that he does count the dead in any battle, even if he leaves the battle off stage in *King Lear*. Othello moderates the horror of murdering his innocent wife by justifying himself as one who has 'loved not wisely but too well' (*Othello*, 5.2.387). If you stopped to recognize the deaths of your soldiers from France, you might justify yourself with the same words, claiming your love for your father. But Othello's wife is still dead and so are your soldiers.

* * *

When you say to Lear, once he finally acts truly as your father, that you have 'No cause' against him (4.6.80), those words are the emotional pinnacle of the play for me. I love you for your forgiveness, your moment of grace. But I see you as being all cause: first when you refuse to make public declaration of your love, and later when you return to assert your father's right, as you call it. Your last words express a wish for those sisters to see you as the *true* daughter who cares for your father and theirs, unto the depths of prison. Was that always your cause?

If I imagine your dying moment in that prison, I hear you echoing Edmund, saying *Cordelia was beloved* with the implication that your sisters were not. You show to what lengths people will go to prove how much they loved and were loved. You frighten me more than your sisters do, because the dangers you represent are more seductive. Yet you embody grace.

To Lear

Your 'darker purpose' sets loose chaos by commanding performances of love. Your life has led you to confuse love with fealty; what happens will teach you differences. By the time you realize that fealty is what's given to a dog in office, too much destruction is already in motion; it's beyond your control. In your final repetitions of *Never* I hear you recognizing as much about your own past as foreseeing a future without Cordelia. Her death culminates your terrible self-recognition of the true king you never have been—the hollowness of the image of authority. Scarce wonder you hallucinate that Cordelia still lives. I pity you enough to hope you're convinced.

I can continue to pity you as long as I remember that when you set the destructive plot on its course, you were being no more or less than who your world called you to be: 'every inch a king' (4.5.119). You inherited the stage you play your part on. As that stage collapses under and around you, I identify with your need to ask the great question: 'Who is it that can tell me who I am?' (1.4.203). I am old enough to fear the answer that the Fool gives you: it's our fate to fade into becoming shadows of ourselves. But your story reminds me that we have choices in how we live this fate, especially in what we ask, or demand, from our children, and in what we give to them.

I believe you never give up the despotic fantasy of your right that whatever the question, you can will your own answers into truth. Your endurance of will is as astonishing as the effects of what you will are appalling. Instead of asking who you are—which was a demand for recognition as king, not a question—you would have done better to ask whom you could trust to advise you who you ought to be. Kent offers himself in that role, and you dismiss him. Like Cornwall, you fail to trust one who is proven through service to you. At least you don't kill Kent, although you cannot recognize him in disguise as Caius. You need to learn to see feelingly, as Gloucester does. I cannot believe you ever do, even in your howling despair.

*   *   *

My ambivalence toward you is expressed in the word Kent uses in his epitaph for you, when he says that you have *usurped* your life. The verb is layered in significance. Most neutrally, usurped means that you had already used more of life than you were either entitled to or wanted to live. But in Shakespeare, echoes of words demand attention, and we still recall Goneril's 'My fool usurps my body' (4.2.30). *Usurp* also means to wrongfully appropriate something; in Shakespeare's history plays, a usurper takes someone else's crown. Beginning with your botched abdication, you usurped the king you yourself had been until then, replacing him with Lear's shadow.

*   *   *

You are one of Shakespeare's few characters who comes close to specifying your age, 'Fourscore and upward' (4.6.64), and you frequently make your age the basis of an appeal for others' patience, the quality you yourself so consistently lack. But in my reading, what matters is not that your own years are many, but that your world is worn out. Your political speeches recognize the vicious pretences of power. Those speeches may be framed in madness, but in them you are most the king I want you to be. You show the potential of the authority that Kent attributes to you— but time has run out.

You may best be my companion when in the storm you recognize the 'Poor naked wretches' and say your most morally self-conscious line: 'I have ta'en / Too little care of this!' (3.4.35–6). When I ask myself your question, *Who is it that can tell me who I am?*, you remind me how I too am one of those who has taken too little care. In the lucid madness of your truth telling, I feel justly accused of my passive participation in the violences and cruelties that my world regrets but accepts as unavoidable aspects of our present dispensation.

You finally beg forgiveness and by a miracle of grace you find it. But then you and Cordelia risk what you have found; you fight a final battle to restore what you have already seen to be a show depending on furred gowns backed by barking dogs. You could have pled with Cordelia to retreat, taking you with her back to France. Either you believe that you alone can be the authority that Kent claims to see in your countenance—an authority people need, to secure their lives—or else fighting is what someone who is every inch a king must do. What, your shadow asks me, has my world made me to be, in my certainty of what I must do?

*   *   *

We return to the beginning, when you responded to Cordelia's silence by telling her nothing comes of nothing. If you could see your story whole, as I see it, would you believe everything comes from nothing? Or would that remain one mystery too far for you? Everything also returns to nothing, and that's all right. God's spies watch the cycles of emergence and return, and the universe needs their watching.

CODA

In Place of the Jig

We need a final breathing out, a moment to enact life going on, not just to say it. The Globe Theatre preserves an Elizabethan performance tradition that's rare in theatres today. At the end of each play, the actors perform a jig: those who have been lying dead on the stage rise up, some are suddenly holding musical instruments, and everyone dances. Those who have recently been set against each other now link arms as fellow players, half in character but with adversity forgotten. I wish this book could end with a jig. Especially after a tragedy, everybody needs to dance.

To read *King Lear* as I have is to hope that in my own unpredictable future and in yours, these words, this story, and these characters might return to us. What will return, when and how, are all part of the unpredictability. If Shakespeare's characters cease to say things I had not expected, that is one way my reading can fail.

Shakespeare's art is to surprise us with how bottomless it is. He reminds us that life will surprise us, other people should surprise us, and we can surprise ourselves. When we do not like how we are surprised—as much of the time we won't—Shakespeare can help us to make that into a liveable story, seeing others as the players they must be and discovering how to play our part among them. For players we are, every one, on this great stage of fools. Knowing that is consolation.

King Lear's consolations are dark. We remember: the worst is not while we can still say it; the worst lies beyond being able to say. This side of that worst, Shakespeare offers us words we hold in memory, characters who accompany us, and a story in which we can dream for a while, and then awake to know our lives anew.

NOTES

Line references to *King Lear* are from the Royal Shakespeare Company edition, edited by Jonathan Bate and Eric Rasmussen (The Modern Library, 2009), except quotations from the 1608 Quarto version that are from The Oxford Shakespeare edition of *King Lear*, edited by Stanley Wells (Oxford, 2001). Quotations to other plays are from the RSC *William Shakespeare: Complete Works*, edited by Bate and Rasmussen (Macmillan, 2007). Among other editions, I especially benefitted from The Arden Shakespeare edition, Third Series, edited by R. A. Foakes (Bloomsbury, 1997).

Chapter 1

1. Emma Smith, *This Is Shakespeare: How to Read the World's Greatest Playwright*. Penguin Random House, 2019, p. 210.
2. Dominic Dromgoole, *Hamlet Globe to Globe: Two Years, 190,000 Miles, 197 Countries, One Play*. Grove Press, 2017, 261.

Chapter 2

1. Translations from Gia-Fu Feng and Jane English, *Tao Te Ching*. Vintage, 1989 and Ursula Le Guin, *Tao Te Ching*. Shambhala, 1997. My thinking on *nothing* is influenced by the writings of David Hinton, most recently *China Root: Taoism, Ch'an and Original Zen*. Shambhala, 2020.

Chapter 3

1. Smith, *This Is Shakespeare*, p. 230.
2. S.L. Goldberg, *An Essay on King Lear*. Cambridge University Press, 1974, p. 185.

Chapter 4

1. *The Dhammapada*. Gil Fronsdal, translator. Shambhala, 2005.

Chapter 5

1. Eve Best, 'A Star Danced' in *Shakespeare and Me,* Susannah Carson, editor. Oneworld, 2014, p. 379.
2. Jan Kott, *Shakespeare Our Contemporary.* Anchor Books, 1966, p. 147.
3. Kott, *Shakespeare Our Contemporary,* pp. 145–6.

Chapter 6

1. On Geoffrey's tale and the 1594 *King Leir,* see Stanley Wells, Introduction, *King Lear.* The Oxford Shakespeare, 2000.

Chapter 7

1. Rowan Williams, *The Tragic Imagination.* Oxford, 2016, pp. 53, 114.
2. Kott, *Shakespeare Our Contemporary,* p. 161.
3. Williams, *The Tragic Imagination,* pp. 155, 118–19.
4. Williams, *The Tragic Imagination,* p. 144.
5. Williams, *The Tragic Imagination,* p. 143.
6. Williams, *The Tragic Imagination,* p. 144.
7. Williams, *The Tragic Imagination,* p. 144.

Chapter 8

1. Harriet Walter, Two Loves, Or the Eternal Triangle, in Carson, ed., *Shakespeare and Me,* p. 395.
2. Jane Smiley, Odd Man Out, in Carson, ed., *Shakespeare and Me,* p. 410.
3. Translation from David Hinton, *Tao Te Ching.* Counterpoint, 2002, verse 78.

SELECTED ADDITIONAL READING

Amanda Anderson, Rita Felski, and Toril Moi, *Character: Three Inquiries in Literary Criticism*. University of Chicago, 2019.

Jonathan Bate, *Soul of the Age: A Biography of the Mind of William Shakespeare*. Random House, 2009.

Harold Bloom, *Lear: The Great Image of Authority*. Scribners, 2018.

Kenneth Burke, *Kenneth Burke on Shakespeare*, S. L. Newstok, editor. Parlor Press, 2007.

Stanley Cavell, *Disowning Knowledge in Seven Plays of Shakespeare*. Cambridge University Press, 2003.

Simon Critchley and Jameson Webster, *The Hamlet Doctrine*. Verso, 2013. (Reissued as *Stay Illusion!*)

Philip Davis, *Reading for Life*. Oxford, 2020.

Ewan Fernie, *Shakespeare for Freedom: Why the Plays Matter*. Cambridge University Press, 2017.

Northrop Frye, *Northrop Frye's Writings on Shakespeare and the Renaissance*, T. Y. Grande and G. Sherbert, editors. University of Toronto Press, 2010.

Marjorie Garber, *Shakespeare After All*. Anchor Books, 2004.

René Girard, *A Theater of Envy: William Shakespeare*. St Augustine's Press, 1991.

Stephen Greenblatt, *Learning to Curse: Essays in Early Modern Culture*. Routledge, 1992.

Frank Kermode, editor. *Shakespeare: King Lear. A Selection of Critical Essays*. Macmillan, 1969.

Maynard Mack, *King Lear in Our Time*. University of California Press, 1965.

Toril Moi, *Revolution of the Ordinary: Literary Studies after Wittgenstein, Austin, and Cavell*. University of Chicago, 2017.

A. D. Nuttall, *Shakespeare the Thinker*. Yale University Press, 2007.

Simon Palfrey, *Poor Tom: Living King Lear*. University of Chicago Press, 2014.

James Shapiro, *The Year of Lear: Shakespeare in 1606*. Simon and Schuster, 2015.

ACKNOWLEDGEMENTS

Philip Davis invited me to participate in the *My Reading* series and patiently read the first drafts, encouraging me to write a book that truly was my reading. I don't know if this is yet the book he wanted, but it would not have its present form without his friendship and guidance. Philip's insights into how people read have informed my thinking throughout.

My old and constant friend David Morris suggested further changes. Comments from Oxford's anonymous reader both encouraged me and suggested necessary revisions.

The final editing was done with my friend Anna Fenton-Hathaway, whose abilities border on the uncanny. My career has been graced with many fine editors, but none have Anna's ear for what I'm trying to express, but have not yet succeeded in saying. There's scarcely a page that she has not touched and improved.

At Oxford, thanks to the series editor, Jacqueline Norton, and to Aimee Wright, who managed this book specifically. Thanks also to Dawn Preston and Bhavani Govindasamy for manuscript preparation; Bhavani's organization and scheduling were exemplary.

To thank my daughters, Stewart Hamilton Frank and Kate Frank, let me say that we write to leave behind what we believe is a better part of ourselves, that those whom we love most may know us as we want to be known.

My father, Arthur W. Frank, Jr., may well live to see the publication of this book. Suffice it to say I would not have read *King Lear* as I do without him. But unlike Lear, his unqualified encouragement of this book has been one of his many gifts.

Finally, to my wife, Cathie Foote, who was both helper and witness to my father's care. Cathie first got me to the Globe, and she has lived with me through what must be lived through, to write this sort of book.

INDEX

This index refers to both the print and digital editions. As a result, many of the indexed terms that span two pages (e.g., 52–3) occur on only one of those pages, in either the print or digital edition.